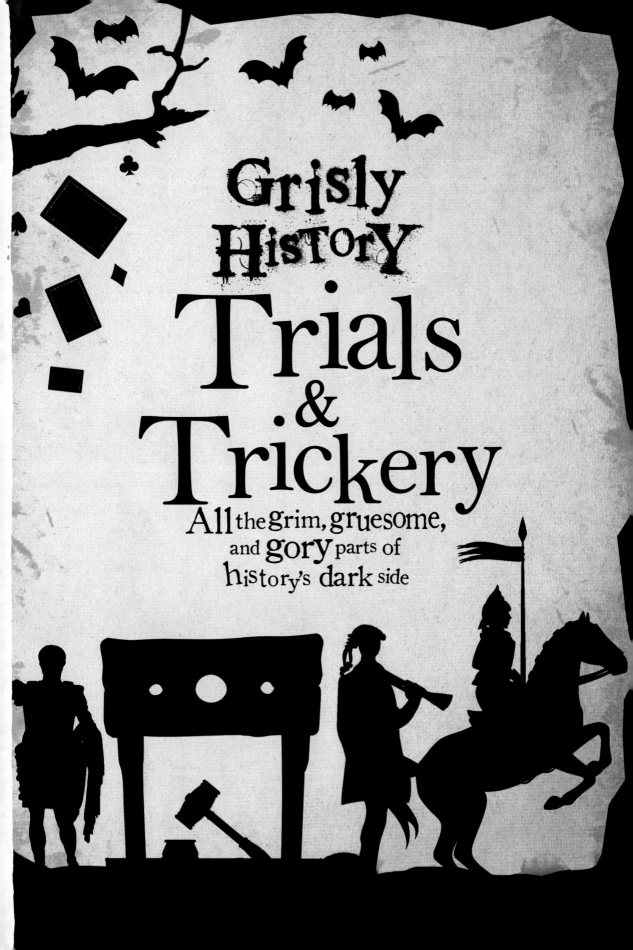

GRISLY HISTORY
Trials & Trickery

All the grim, gruesome, and gory parts of history's dark side

WeldonOwen

PUBLISHING

First published in Great Britain in 2016 by Weldon Owen,
an imprint of the Bonnier Publishing Group.
Kings Road Publishing
3.08 The Plaza, 535 King's Road
Chelsea, London, SW10 0SZ

© 2016 Weldon Owen. All rights reserved.
www.weldonowen.co.uk
www.bonnierpublishing.co.uk

ISBN: 978-178342-257-9

First Edition
2 4 6 8 10 9 7 5 3 1

Printed in China

Grisly History

Trials & Trickery

All the grim, gruesome, and gory parts of history's dark side

Sandra Lawrence

WeldonOwen
PUBLISHING

CONTENTS

Trials & Trickery

Most people agree there are some things you just don't do – stealing, for example, or murder. But what *is* murder? It's not always as clear-cut as a crazy axeman on a dark night…

From the very earliest civilizations, people have tried to figure out what was important to them and created laws that would keep those values. If someone was thought to have broken the law, important people in the community would decide whether they had done the deed, if they should be punished, and if so, what that punishment should be.

Sometimes it was the king or leader of the society. It might be a group of people or a religious body.

Most societies believe that someone is innocent until they've been proven guilty and that it's up to the accuser to prove the person they are accusing is guilty. How do you go about proving that, though? What if the method chosen isn't fair? What *is* fair?

Trial by jury, where a group of people decide the fate of the accused, goes back as far as ancient Greece and Rome, but juries have not always been made up of "peers" – fellow citizens chosen at random from ordinary people. They have been appointed by kings or the Church, or have even chosen themselves. That last one rarely worked out well…

To modern eyes, some of the ways people "tried" each other in the past seems rather odd. Maybe if they could see us today, they'd be just as bemused!

Take trial by combat. The accuser and the accused would literally fight it out on the battlefield in a hand-to-hand duel. The winner clearly had God on his side, so he must have been in the right! Sometimes rich people who thought they might lose the battle would appoint a "champion" to fight for them, but if you were poor, you'd better have big muscles!

Trial by ordeal would seem just as crazy to us now. The accused would have to go through some horrible experience and, depending on how they came out of it, would be judged innocent or guilty. They might have to plunge their hand into boiling water to retrieve a stone or a ring. Perhaps they'd be forced to walk over red-hot ploughshares (metal blades) or hold a scalding-hot iron rod. Absolute innocence would be proven if they had no injury at all, but since that rarely happened, they were allowed to wrap up the wound. If it had healed sufficiently a few days later, they were declared innocent.

Sometimes people were tied up and thrown into water. If they floated, they were innocent; if they sank, they were guilty. In the sixteenth and seventeenth centuries, this was reversed – if you floated, then obviously you were a witch, because everyone knew water rejects the guilty!

Trickery can take many forms, from personal betrayal to treason against one's country. Sometimes people betray their country because they truly believe their leaders are doing the wrong thing. They might commit treason for religious reasons, family loyalty, money, or even love. Some of the worst punishments have traditionally been reserved for treason, and even today, traitors are generally despised.

History has thrown up a whole bunch of twisted ways people have messed with the law. Good people who turned bad; bad people who turned even worse. Citizens who sold their countries; countries who sold their citizens. It could have been evil individuals or evil groups. Or it just could have been evil times.

The law has been just as easily warped. Corrupt trials, foul ways of making people confess – perhaps even to things they never thought or did – sadistic ways of punishing people, and sordid methods of disposing of them.

There's no room in this book to cover all the hideous deeds in the world's grisly history, but hey – you have to start somewhere. Cover your eyes, folks, and never let what happens within these pages ever happen again.

THE BETRAYAL OF JESSE JAMES

3 APRIL, 1882

You might think outlaws would stick together, but treachery happens everywhere, even among thieves. And somehow it's worse when the betrayer is your friend.

Old-timers spin yarns of derring-do and dastardly desperados out there in the Wild West. To hear about them, Billy the Kid, Doc Holliday, and Belle Starr sound almost like heroes. Anyone at the wrong end of the James Gang's rifles, however, didn't find them quite so romantic.

RUSSELVILLE BANK ROBBERY.

The robbery of Southern Deposit Bank in Russellville, Kentucky, of $12,000 on 20 March 1868, has been attributed to the Jesse James and Younger brothers gangs.

Those James boys should have known better. Their daddy was a preacher, though he took off to find gold when they were small fries and never came back. Frank and little brother Jesse went off to fight in the American Civil War and joined a brutal local militia called Quantrill's Raiders. They got a taste for the nastiest kind of violence and figured they could continue the hobby after the war.

In 1866, Frank and Jesse staged the first-ever daylight bank robbery and netted around $60,000.

For fifteen years the notorious James brothers robbed banks, held up stagecoaches, derailed trains, and killed people throughout Kansas and Missouri. Jesse was a colourful character. Folks said he saluted his victims and even tipped his hat to the ladies. There were whispers that he was the American Robin Hood, giving away his loot to the poor, though there's no evidence he ever shared anything with anyone.

Frank retired and Jesse got a new gang. There was a price on their heads, though, and the bounty hunters were moving in. They say Jesse planned to give up crime too, but wanted to stage one last robbery. He only trusted two men – his friends Charles and Robert Ford.

Bad Move, Jesse

The Ford brothers had been plotting with the local governor, dazzled by the massive reward for Jesse's capture.

It was a hot day. Jesse had eaten breakfast and had taken off his coat, waistcoat, and guns. He noticed a dusty picture over the fireplace and got on a chair to clean it. Bob Ford saw his chance. He drew his gun and fired.

Robert Ford

Young Robert Ford idolized Jesse James. He'd read what James had done in the war, and loved the stories he'd heard about his hero's life as an outlaw. Bob's older brother Charles got in with the James gang, and when Jesse went solo, Bob was invited to join him. He enjoyed the robbing and the shooting, but life on the run was tough.

When the Missouri governor, Thomas T. Crittenden, offered the Fords $10,000 and a full pardon for the death of the most wanted criminal in America, killing James seemed like a good way out for Bob. No one knows why Bob shot his hero in the back; perhaps he just couldn't look him in the eye.

Things went sour almost immediately. Instead of being rewarded, Charles and Bob Ford were charged with murder. They escaped hanging two hours after their sentence but only received a tiny fraction of the reward they were promised.

"The Coward" Robert Ford shot Jesse James in the back as he cleaned a photoframe above the fireplace.

Jesse James

Jesse James knew exactly why everyone thought he was the baddest cat in town: it was because he'd told them. He was the first outlaw to leave a press release about how fantastic he was at the scene of his crimes. He even had a spin doctor, someone who cleverly manipulates the news.

James and the editor of the *Kansas City Times,* John Newman Edwards, cooked up an image that made the dangerous gangster look like a folk hero. By the time Edwards had finished, Jesse James was practically sitting with King Arthur at the round table and sharing tales of gallantry with Robin Hood.

James made sure he looked the part, too, dressing sharply and always saving a wink for the ladies. No one can agree how he lost the tip of his finger, though some say that's how he got his nickname, "Dingus" – he apparently shot it off by accident and shouted that word instead of swearing! He always wore gloves so he couldn't be identified by his lack of digits.

According to Robert Ford, James realized he been betrayed when he read in the newspaper about another gang member turning himself in, and wondered why Ford hadn't told him.

Pinkerton

One of the reasons Governor Crittenden was so eager for the Ford brothers to rid him of Jesse James was that the famous Pinkerton National Detective Agency, founded in 1850, had totally failed to do the job.

The agency took on the James Gang case and immediately started losing detectives. One, John Witcher, was found dead, shot in the stomach.

Allan Pinkerton made it his personal mission to track down the James boys, and in 1875, a group of agents threw a bomb into the James family farmhouse. The outlaws weren't home, but their nine-year-old half-brother was killed and their mother lost an arm.

This meant war. Anyone who had helped the detectives was relentlessly intimidated. One neighbour was killed. There was no mistaking it now – those James boys were trouble.

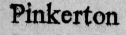
A gang of agents threw a bomb into the James family farmhouse.

Cashing In

Everyone wanted a piece of Jesse's story. His old man sold "pebbles from his grave" at a quarter each. His son, Jesse Junior, starred in two heavily romanticized silent movies about his dad, and Robert Ford – well, he tried to cash in on his part in the sorry tale.

He and Charles toured the West, re-enacting the event and posing for photos, but the public hated it. Bob had shot his friend in the back in his own home, which they thought a pretty low-down, cowardly thing to do, forgetting that they'd been the ones who wanted James stopped in the first place!

Ford never got away from the incident. Even his gravestone says "The Man Who Shot Jesse James".

Bit Coins, Wild West Style

The main reason for being an outlaw (apart from the kick of knowing you were the most evil guy in town) was the cash. A national banking system was being set up, but people were suspicious of "greenbacks" – paper money. You knew where you stood with a nice lump of gold.

A double eagle was a $20 gold piece. A single eagle was worth $10. There were also smaller coins called half and quarter eagles.

"Bits" were leftovers from the old pirate favourites, "pieces of eight" – literally "bits" of old Spanish money. One bit was an eighth of a peso. There weren't actually any "bit" coins minted, but a dime was close enough, which was called "two bits". Shave and a haircut, anyone?

A. SMITH & WESSON REVOLVER

will make a hole in a $10. bill. But it's worth all you pay for it.

Revolvers never disappoint.

17 Stockbridge St.,
SPRINGFIELD, - - MASS.

Guns

Every outlaw had a gun. Jesse had several, including a Colt .45 "Peacemaker", one of the most famous guns of all time. It was a revolver, but as a single action weapon, you had to fully cock the hammer before pulling the trigger. Some gunslingers held down the trigger with one hand and "fanned" the hammer with the other hand to make it shoot really fast. The method wasn't very accurate, but folks still got out of the way pretty darn quick.

Bob Ford shot Jesse James with a nickel-plated Smith & Wesson .44 Model 3 revolver, also known as a Schofield because of improvements made to it by Major George Schofield. It was toted by Pat Garrett, Billy the Kid, and Wyatt Earp. Jesse also had one; some say the gun that killed him was once his own.

A Grave Mistake

Jesse was buried in the James family farm's front yard to deter grave robbers. His epitaph read "Murdered April 3, 1882, by a Traitor and Coward Whose Name Is Not Worthy to Appear Here". He was later moved to Mount Olivet Cemetery in Kearney, Missouri.

In 1948, however, a very elderly man named J. Frank Dalton came forward, claiming he was the real Jesse James. He said he'd faked his own death and had lived quietly in Texas ever since. He died in 1951 at age 103 and was buried in Granbury Cemetery. DNA tests have proven that James really is in Kearney, but J. Frank Dalton's Granbury grave still claims to contain the outlaw himself.

The Man Who Killed the Man Who Killed Jesse James

"Hello, Bob".

Just as Jesse James had had his back turned when he was shot, Robert Ford wasn't facing the man who shot him. As Ford turned to see who was speaking, Edward O'Kelley, a dangerous local ne'er-do-well, gave him the benefit of both barrels from his shotgun.

Some say it was in revenge for James' death; others think it was an argument over a gold ring. But no one really knows why O'Kelley did it. It surely couldn't be just so his gravestone would read "The Man Who Killed the Man Who Killed Jesse James"?

JOAN OF ARC

*If you're going to go down, go down fighting.
After all, God is on your side...*

She'd been incarcerated for a year, constantly interrogated and taunted by her male guards. Yet in court, Jehanne la Pucelle, aka Joan the Maid, aka Joan of Arc, ran rings around her English accusers, calmly stating she was innocent and answering questions designed to trap her with clever, simple statements. It should have been easy. She was just nineteen, illiterate... a peasant, for heaven's sake. They'd charged her with seventy offenses, from horse stealing to witchcraft, but they just couldn't trip her up.

Joan rode into battle on her white horse.

She'd tried to escape, jumping sixty feet off a tower, knocking herself out, and getting badly bruised. She couldn't have expected to *live*, could she? How about adding "attempted suicide" to the charges? Better chain her to a block in case she tried any more funny business.

She became ill. That would never do. They couldn't have her dying *before* she was found guilty.

They were getting nowhere. They'd torture her, if they thought for a moment it might work.

Hang on – what about the clothes she was wearing? Men's clothes, tightly bound with dozens of cords in the hope the guards couldn't untie them to attack her. Dressing as a man went against nature itself! Surely there must be something in the Bible against it...

It had all been so different just a couple of years ago. Joan had travelled across enemy territory over eleven nights, wearing men's clothing for safety. When she reached the royal court, the crown prince had given her a full set of gleaming armour, a white horse to ride, and an army to lead against the English. No one had suggested she dress as a girl then.

Joan was shown the stake in the marketplace. Spooked, she signed a confession denying she'd ever had guidance from God. A few days later, though, she was back in trousers. Some whispered darkly that the only garments given to her were men's clothes.

On 30 May 1431, the Maid was burned at the stake in the marketplace at Rouen. Even the jubilant English and suspicious churchmen knew it wasn't the last they'd hear of Joan of Arc.

It took almost 500 years for her to be officially canonized, but to the French people, the Maid of Orléans almost immediately became "Saint" Joan.

Joan

The Hundred Years War between England, France, and various other states was in full flow. The old king, Charles VI, suffered schizophrenic episodes, causing his nobles to fight among themselves for power. The English king, Henry V, had taken advantage of the chaos, and much of northern France was now under English control. Domrémy, the village where Joan was born, was frequently raided.

Joan started hearing voices at age thirteen. Devoutly religious, she fervently believed they were sent from God and that she had a mission: to save France, overthrow her enemies, and crown the dauphin (prince) as Charles VII of France.

She took a vow of chastity. When her father found her a husband, Joan, now sixteen, refused to marry. Instead she travelled to a nearby stronghold of Prince Charles de Valois, where the local magistrate, Robert de Baudricourt, kept turning her away. She was already gaining fans, though, many of whom remembered an old prophecy saying a virgin would save France. Could this girl be the Chosen One?

Eventually the magistrate gave in. Joan cropped her hair, dressed as a boy, and went to Chinon, and Charles' court.

Joan's Sword and Banner

Although the dauphin offered Joan a sword, the Maid's voices told her that behind an altar in a church about 250 miles away, *her* weapon awaited her.

For many years, returning knights had left their swords in the little church at Sainte-Catherine-de-Fierbois as a tribute to the martyr. One of those knights was Charles Martel, grandfather of the great king Charlemagne, and it was his sword Joan had set her sights on.

She told clerics it would be rusty, with five crosses on it. They found it where she said it would be, and the rust fell away easily. She was given sheaths for it of red velvet and gold cloth, but she had a more practical one in mind, of good, strong, honest leather.

She loved her banner even more, carrying it into battle to inspire the troops. It was white and embroidered with the words "Jhesus Maria" and images of lilies, two angels, and Jesus Christ.

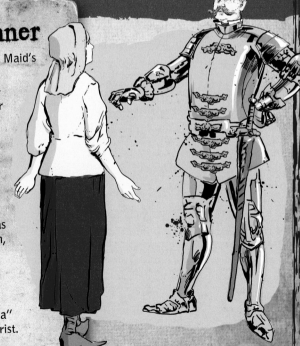

Joan visited her local magistrate, Robert de Baudricourt.

Dauphin

Crown Prince Charles de Valois was in a pickle. Although he was the official heir to the throne, he couldn't actually get to Reims to be crowned.

Despite the crowded room, Joan recognized Charles instantly and marched up to him. She revealed secrets to the sceptical prince that only God – or God's messenger – could know. She promised she'd see him crowned king and asked for an army. His counselors said no way; Charles said yes.

Joan's army set off for the besieged city of Orléans, where Joan inspired several attacks, forcing the English to retreat. She was a hero.

The dauphin was crowned Charles VII in 1429. Joan, however, was making powerful enemies. The English and Burgundians thought she was a witch. The Church didn't like her, either – nobody should be able to speak with God or his saints except through them! Charles' jealous courtiers just thought she was getting far too powerful.

Joan wanted to take Paris, but Charles' advisors hung back. In the hesitation, the Anglo-Burgundians reinforced the city.

In 1430, Joan was thrown from her horse and captured by the Burgundians. They took her to the castle of Bouvreuil at Rouen, occupied by the English. The French did not stop them.

The Voices

Many people have tried to explain the voices Joan heard – everything from schizophrenia to epilepsy has been suggested. She named three saints: Michael, Catherine, and Margaret. At her trial, she said she saw bright lights at the same time, which some believe could imply migraines or a neurological disorder. Some theories even put forward bipolar disease or bovine TB, which in rare cases can cause seizures. Oddly, she always retained her faculties of reason, which is something many people with these ailments lose. Her answers at the trial were always lucid and clever.

Whether she suffered from mental or physical illness, or really did hear messages from the saints, her story remains one of the most powerful of the Middle Ages.

Injuries

Although Joan didn't do any actual fighting, she was injured twice in battle. She took an arrow in the shoulder helping to raise a siege ladder at Orléans and a crossbow bolt in her leg trying to liberate Paris. Both were nasty physical injuries, but symbolically they were much worse.

Until then, people had believed she was invincible, protected by God. When God "allowed" her to be hurt, even though she had actually predicted the wounds, she became "human" again and suddenly wasn't any more important than anyone else.

Joan took an arrow in the shoulder while helping to raise a seige ladder.

A Thorough Job

Joan was actually burned three times. She asked for a cross to be held in front of her as she died and kept another inside her dress, next to her heart.

The English were already nervous about her symbolic power to the French, and despite their claiming she was a witch, they had nagging doubts, and some thought she could actually be holy. The last thing they wanted were any bits left over that might hold magical powers as relics. They burned the remains twice more until they were ashes and dumped them into the river Seine.

The executioner, Geoffroy Thérage, was particularly worried, later admitting he feared damnation for killing a saint.

Joan of Arc was burned at the stake; her executioner admitting that he feared that he had killed a saint.

Records

Nearly 600 years after Joan's death, we can be pretty sure what went on at her trial. Three court officials took extensive notes in French and wrote them up in Latin. Five copies were made, and three of them still exist.

We also have records of the retrial that took place twenty years after her death. Additional details emerge showing how the first trial, if not exactly rigged, was certainly highly political.

Will the Real Joan of Arc Step Forward?

After Joan's death, several women claimed to be the "real" Joan after having miraculously escaped from the fire and whisked away via a secret passage. One of them, Jeanne (aka Claude) des Armoises, it is said, even had the support of Joan's brothers. She'd "been in hiding" and married a knight. She must have been convincing because wherever she travelled, people "recognized" her, inviting her to swanky receptions and giving her presents. Then, according to one source, she met the king. Charles asked her the godly secret he and Joan had shared, and Claude collapsed, begging for mercy.

CHARLES I OF ENGLAND

30 JANUARY 1649

It's been nine years of civil war. Thousands of people have died in villages, towns, and cities across the land. The king has finally been captured ...

Some whispered the king should be quietly done away with. Poisoning, perhaps, or even a straightforward assassination. Parliament knew, however, that the honour of the new regime was at stake. This had to be done right. There must be a trial.

King Charles I reigned for twenty-three years, ten months and four days.

The courtroom was open to all; there wasn't a seat left in the house. Tensions were so high that the man presiding had his hat reinforced with steel plates in case of trouble.

King Charles I sat with his hat on, too, a mark of his disrespect for the court. When he was charged with treason, he laughed, refusing to acknowledge the court's right to try him. He refused to speak further, so he was taken away and found guilty anyway. Fifty-nine men signed his death warrant.

Charles was spared the usual traitor's death of hanging, drawing, and quartering, sentenced to beheading instead.

Two days before the execution, he was allowed to see his youngest children, thirteen-year-old Elizabeth and eight-year-old Henry, for the last time.

On the morning of 30 January 1649, Charles dressed with care, asking for an extra shirt so he wouldn't shiver from cold and appear to be afraid. He drank a glass of claret, ate some bread, and popped an orange stuck with cloves in his pocket for later.

He walked from St. James Palace to Banqueting House, pausing to point out a tree his brother had planted years beforehand. He was taken upstairs, where he had to wait four hours, as the scaffold wasn't ready.

No one would have heard the king's words in the racket that erupted when he finally stepped out. By all accounts the conversation was very polite, given he was about to have his head chopped off. Charles asked the executioner if his hair would get in the way; the headsman asked him to put it up, so he called for a satin bonnet. Then, still convinced of his divine right to rule, he announced, "I go from a corruptible to an incorruptible Crown".

The executioner needed just one blow. The ex-king's head was displayed to the crowd, and his body was carried away in a velvet coffin. Some people dipped their handkerchiefs in Charles' blood, either as trophies of victory or as the holy relics of a martyr.

King Charles I walked from St. James Palace to Banqueting House.

Banqueting House

London's Palace of Whitehall was as sumptuous as it was gigantic. Charles I had commissioned the painter Rubens to decorate its magnificent Banqueting House, where he held court masques and entertained ambassadors. A few years later, the king would step out of one of its windows onto a hastily erected wooden scaffold to be executed.

Most of Whitehall burned down in the seventeenth century, but the Banqueting House survived. Every January the Society of King Charles the Martyr holds a memorial service there. The English Civil War Society organizes a commemorative march on the route the king took on that last morning and lays a wreath at the execution site.

Charles I

Charles had been brought up to believe he had a divine right to rule. He was in charge because God said so. Some thought his very touch could cure a nasty disease called scrofula, or "the King's Evil". The power went to his head, but sadly, his decisions didn't always live up to the hype.

He upset everyone – the Protestants by actually falling in love with his Roman Catholic wife, the Scots by trying to impose Church of England views, prominent nobles by running wars very badly, and Parliament because people weren't allowed even basic rights, like not being imprisoned without trial or being taxed willy-nilly whenever the king wanted more cash.

On the plus side, he had exquisite taste. He always dressed well and he collected works of fine art, including a splendid ceiling he commissioned for the Banqueting House. That ceiling was one of the last things he would see.

Charles declared the House of Commons impertinent for wanting to discuss views that weren't his own. Tit-for-tat, the Commons refused the king tax revenue for anything longer than a year. The king was outraged and dissolved Parliament. He dug up ancient laws allowing him to tax obscure things, sold off monopolies, and started forcing towns to pay a special levy "to build ships".

Incredibly, he couldn't see that this might make him unpopular.

Oliver Cromwell

Cavaliers are often depicted as having ringlet curls and wearing lacy cuffs.

Oddly, Oliver Cromwell, like Charles, believed God had chosen him to perform His will. They couldn't both be right.

Both men were driven by strong religious convictions, but while Charles came from a traditional High Church, Cromwell was a Puritan. His faith was simple, without frills or argument. To him, concentrating on the Bible was the most important thing, and any kind of fun or fancy distracted the mind from God. He even insisted his portrait was exact – including all his warts – rather than flattering, like most people of the time.

That's not to say he didn't allow the occasional lively gathering – his daughter's wedding was quite a party – but for him, the sheer extravagance at court proved the king needed to go.

Cromwell joined the Parliamentarian army and was quickly promoted, rising to become leader of the "Roundheads" and eventually, the country, as Lord Protector. It's worth remembering that he, like Charles, closed Parliament when it disagreed with him.

He remains a controversial figure, celebrated by some, hated by others. The man wasn't without a heart, though. He later admitted watching the doomed king play with his children and, being a family man himself, weeping.

Cavaliers and Roundheads

Popular imagination sees the Royalist "Cavalier" as having a head of ringlet curls and wearing lacy cuffs and bucket-top boots, while they see the Parliamentarian "Roundheads" as miserable fellows with pudding-bowl haircuts and leather "buff coats". In truth, there was very little difference between the way most of them looked. Rank-and-file "pikemen" would have had very basic clothes, and musketeers would have worn leather jerkins to deflect stray sparks.

Officers on both sides were often pretty fancy dressers. Not all Parliamentarians were Puritans; some just believed in the right for Parliament to have a say. They had no problem with wearing as many lace collars, fancy gloves, and feathers in their hats as the Royalists. Cromwell's New Model Army's uniform included red coats and metal helmets.

Executioner

We don't know who actually beheaded the king. The executioner and his assistant were masked and wore false hair and beards. It was usual to brandish a severed head with the words ''Behold the head of a traitor!'' but Charles' head was held aloft in silence to disguise the headsman's voice.

Richard Brandon, Common Hangman of London, was used to executing upper-class folk and commoners alike, but even he was squeamish at the idea of killing a king and turned down the job. A ''confession'' published after his death admitted he'd relented and was paid £30 for the service, but many said it was a forgery. Whoever did it was a pro. In 1813, the king's body was exhumed and examined. The fatal strike had been a single, clean blow.

The King was killed with a single, clean blow.

Oliver Cromwell's head was stuck on a pike at Westminster Hall.

Death to the Regicides

On the death of Oliver Cromwell, the Commonwealth faltered as his son Richard ''Tumbledown Dick'' abdicated. Triumphant, Charles II returned from exile, but even as the citizens cheered, the dancing began, and the theatres reopened, thirty-one men were hurriedly packing their bags. The remaining commissioners who had signed Charles I's death warrant knew his son would want revenge.

Some ''regicides'' fled to America and continental Europe, chased by Charles II's spies. Of those caught, the fortunate were imprisoned for life. The rest were hanged, drawn, and quartered, the traditional traitor's punishment.

Even Oliver Cromwell didn't escape, despite being dead. His corpse was dug up and ''put on trial'' for treason. It was found guilty and ''hanged'' at Tyburn, and the head was stuck on a spike at Westminster Hall.

Cancelled Christmas

Puritans believed people should be worshiping God. Jolly pastimes distracted a person from reading the Bible. Dancing, going to the theatre, and drinking excessively were unseemly. You could be put in the stocks for working on a Sunday, and if you did anything other than go to church on that day, you were considered a bad person.

Worst of all was the disgraceful practice known as Christmas. People loved Christmas. They sang songs, decorated their houses, watched plays, ate mince pies, exchanged gifts, and played practical jokes on each other instead of spending the day soberly sitting in church.

In 1644, celebrating ''holy days'' was banned by Parliament. Soldiers went through the streets sniffing for signs of Christmas dinners being cooked and confiscating any goodies they found.

A Spooky Figure

After the execution, Oliver Cromwell granted permission for Charles' family to sew the head back onto his body, embalm him, and even paint his portrait, complete with stitch marks!

Almost immediately the dead king entered into mythology. A story began that while his body lay in state, a hooded figure appeared in the shadows and stood, staring at the corpse. It was heard to mutter ''Cruel necessity'' before disappearing. Those who ''witnessed'' the event said the man's voice and walk were those of Cromwell himself.

Charles was laid to rest at Windsor, near Henry VIII and Jane Seymour. He was later canonized as a saint by the Church of England.

CELEBRITY EXECUTIONERS

Whatever you do, take pride in your work...

The Great Sanson

Charles-Henri Sanson was part of a six-generation dynasty of hangmen, but he is best known as the man who wielded the notorious death machine *la guillotine* during the French Revolution. He hadn't wanted to follow his dad and grampa into the family business, but once he inherited the blood-red coat of Master Executioner, he found he had a flair for it.

He dispatched more than 3,000 people, including King Louis himself, though he couldn't face killing the queen, Marie Antoinette, so he got his son to do it for him.

Sanson was instrumental in introducing the guillotine. He argued that killing so many people at once was hard work, not to mention it kept wearing out his axe.

In his spare time, Sanson liked to dissect his victims, grow herbs, and play the violin.

Meister Franz

Franz Schmidt, a German executioner, had an unusual side-job.

His diary of the 361 people he executed between 1573 and 1617 shows in detail whether he hanged, decapitated, burned, drowned, or broke his victims on the wheel and what they'd been convicted for.

When he got home, however, Schmidt put on a different hat – as a medical healer. From his own calculations, he saw up to 15,000 patients, especially after he retired as hangman of the city of Nuremberg and became a full-time consultant. As is unusual for executioners, "Meister Franz" was popular – when he died, the people gave him a state funeral!

Souflikar

Emperor Mahomet IV's legendary "head gardener" Souflikar had some very special skills indeed. He was particularly good at "pruning" the heads of people the sultan didn't like anymore. He sometimes gave them a sporting chance – he challenged them to a race through the gardens. If they won, he'd let them go.

They never won.

Souflikar is said to have killed at least 5,000 people over five years, an incredible feat, especially when you realize he used no weapons. The unfortunates were all strangled to death with Souflikar's bare hands.

Lady Betty

In 1780, or so historians believe, Elizabeth Dolan from County Kerry, Ireland, was sentenced to hang. She had murdered a stranger for his money, not realizing it was her own son, a sailor who had returned home a rich man.

Elizabeth and twenty-four other condemned criminals were standing on the scaffold, but the town hangman hadn't turned up. Elizabeth shouted, "Spare me, yer Honour, and I'll hang them all!" beginning a long career as "Lady Betty", the scariest executioner in all of Ireland.

Lady Betty enjoyed her work so much that she used to sketch her victims as they dangled. Legend has it that when she died, the walls of her cottage were covered with pictures of hanged people.

Louis Congo

When the French territory of Louisiana needed a public executioner in 1725, they weren't exactly overwhelmed with applicants. They therefore decided to free a slave to do the dirty work and asked one fellow, Louis Congo, if he'd be interested. Congo thought about it and decided he'd rather be free than not – but he was no pushover.

In return for whippings, brandings, torture, and execution, Congo wanted a decent life. He wanted a nice house for himself and his wife, in addition to food and wine and decent pay. Perhaps the only black man allowed to kill a white person, he didn't care what colour his victims were; he treated everyone with the same meticulous cruelty.

A quick flogging earned him £10, while a hanging bagged him £30. If he had to do something gross, like breaking someone on the wheel or burning them alive, he charged more – £40, payable in tobacco. Given that Congo once broke eight people on the wheel in one sitting, his tobacco pouch was definitely packed!

Jack Ketch

Still reviled today as the worst executioner ever, John "Jack" Ketch was terrible at his job. He worked for King Charles II of England, and whether through malice, laziness, or just incompetence, he seemed incapable of cutting off a head cleanly.

James, First Duke of Monmouth, gave him gold to make his death quick, and Ketch still took five attempts to sever the duke's head. The crowd was furious – if he hadn't had an armed guard, Ketch himself might have died that day. He blamed his victims for his poor aim, claiming, for example, that they'd failed to place their head the right way on the block or had distracted him at the last moment!

Even today, the name "Jack Ketch" is sometimes used as another word for executioner or even the devil himself.

WITCHES

Double, double, toil and trouble,
fire burn and cauldron bubble ...

The idea of witchcraft exists in every continent and every society – if we believe in good, then its opposite, evil, must also exist. In times when people couldn't explain diseases, strange weather, and any other kind of bad fortune, they looked around for someone to blame.

Witch "hunts" weren't quite what they sound like. They didn't usually involve search parties with flaming torches and pitchforks, trekking around the countryside, looking for sorcerers dancing around a bonfire. They tended to be courts trying to figure out who was responsible for bad stuff happening in a village. Perhaps milk was curdling, plague had arrived, or crops had failed.

Nearly all witchfinders relied on townsfolk accusing each other. Anyone might be denounced by anyone: neighbours, friends, families. From the oldest man to the youngest child, no one was immune – but most were women, usually middle-aged. Everyone, innocent or guilty, was expected to supply names of other possible witches.

In continental Europe, witchcraft came under the jurisdiction of the Catholic Church, which usually meant the Inquisition. "Witches" were accused of heresy against God, and horrific torture was used to extract a confession.

In other countries, such as England, the court was civil rather than church-based, and the crime was "merely" of "evil deeds". All-out torture wasn't allowed, so the

People secretly accused each other, either because they were caught up in the mania, or because they wanted revenge.

investigators had to be cunning.

Perhaps the victim couldn't recite prayers or long passages from the Bible without stumbling. Well, they must be guilty!

What if the person accusing them got better when they were touched by the "witch"? Guilty!

Suppose the investigator made a cake out of the accused's urine and fed it to their pet dog? When the dog would eat the cake, supposedly the witch would cry out in pain. Ka-ching! Guilty!

People might be weighed against a Bible or other holy items. If they were lighter, they were witches. In Oudewater in the Netherlands, people would deliberately get tested at the local weigh house and buy a certificate to prove they were god-fearing citizens, very handy in case their neighbours decided to accuse them of sorcery later.

"Ducking" was also thought to be a surefire witch-discoverer. The individual was tied to a chair and dumped in the

People were dunked and weighed as tests to see if they were witches.

local pond. If they floated, they'd clearly renounced their baptismal vows. God's pure water had rejected them, and they were guilty. If they sank, they were innocent. In the unfortunate case they accidentally drowned before they could be dragged out, at least their souls would go to heaven.

Were There Actually Witches?

There were a few people in medieval times who followed their own form of spirituality, and it's possible some accused "witches" did practise "sorcery" of some kind. Whether "white magic" or evil spells, it was all heresy as far as the Catholic Church was concerned. Oddly, the term heresy comes from a Greek word for "choice"!

Many admitted to witchcraft – though given the torture, heavy-handed interrogation, and hysteria, the only real surprise is that more people didn't!

Some confessed willingly. They could have had psychological issues or been vulnerable in other ways. In olden times, people who were physically or mentally disabled were often thought to be either stupid, rejected by God, or created by the devil. Many were isolated figures: old, sick, or just plain lonely. Elderly widows were easy targets. The sheer number of "witches" discovered, though, looks suspicious – "witchcraft" was found because people wanted to find it.

People were sometimes accused by young children who'd had a nightmare that the "witch" had done something bad. Worse, they occasionally invented outrageous stories to cover up for their own naughtiness.

Citizens accused people they wanted to get rid of or wreak revenge on. It led to a culture of fear. The witch could be anyone… including the next-door neighbour! Of course the neighbour, in turn, probably had the same thought. Sometimes villagers took matters into their own hands and executed witches, vigilante style.

How Many Died?

The countries of continental Europe usually burned people found guilty of sorcery, though they were occasionally granted the luxury of being strangled first. In other countries, such as England and America, they were hanged instead.

We don't know exact figures, but a conservative estimate puts a total of 90,000 prosecutions in Europe leading to around 45,000 executions, and those are just the ones that came to trial. In America the numbers of accused were fewer, but still in the hundreds.

Folks weren't interested in how many witches they had caught, though. They were more worried by how many remained loose.

Lurid pamphlets described the evil deeds of Satan's worshipers. Woodcuts showed witches boiling children and roasting them, worshiping the devil, trampling on crosses, and turning themselves into animals. No matter that no one had ever actually seen anyone doing that. It was in the press, so it had to be true!

A woodcut of witches with the devil.

The Witchfinder King

King James I was obsessed with witchcraft. While he was still James VI of Scotland, before he took the English throne, he personally interrogated and watched the torture of one woman, Agnes Sampson, until she admitted to all kinds of ridiculous charges.

She confessed she'd baptized a cat and thrown it into the sea attached to human limbs, causing a storm. She'd made a wax model of the king and melted it. She'd tried to procure the king's undergarments so she could smear them with toad poison to make him ill.

She was pronounced guilty of being a witch, strangled to death, and then burned.

When the jury dismissed another woman's case, however, James was livid. He forced them to find her guilty. She was sentenced to death, but she pleaded her belly (see page 43) and was granted a stay of execution. She was later quietly released.

When he became king of England, James was shocked at how liberal the English were and immediately passed a law banning, among other things, the resurrection of corpses for the purposes of witchcraft, murder by sorcery, and making a pact with the devil.

The Witchfinder General

After James, there was less interest in witch-hunting until the English Civil War suddenly turned the whole country upside down.

A man named Matthew Hopkins came forward, claiming every Friday he was disturbed by strange voices outside his window – clearly witches discussing various illegal meetings. He said the evil ones had sent a bear-like spirit to kill him for spying on them, but his pure godliness had protected him from harm.

Over 14 months between 1644 and 1646, Hopkins, his associate John Stearne, and their assistants, called "pricking-women", roamed East Anglia as England's most notorious witchfinders.

Although torture wasn't allowed, Hopkins managed to justify it in the name of exposing evil. He mainly used pricking, ducking, and *tormentum insomniae* – that's sleep deprivation to the rest of us. People were kept awake by force until they'd sign anything.

Hopkins' short reign of terror was responsible for the deaths of around 300 women, mainly by hanging. He was a grisly inspiration for the New World, especially Salem, where his witch-finding methods proved "useful" – and were expanded on in grim style.

The Salem Witch Trials, 1692

Although the most notorious prosecutions and executions in America took place near Salem, Massachusetts, much of seventeenth-century New England was gripped by a hysterical belief that witchcraft was responsible for a series of strange fits experienced by townsfolk, mainly young girls.

In 1692, Elizabeth Parris, age nine, and her eleven-year-old cousin, Abigail Williams, started experiencing weird episodes – much worse than an epileptic fit. They screamed and rolled around on the floor, threw things, and crawled under the furniture, making crazy noises and rolling their eyes. They said they'd been pricked with pins. Soon several other young women started doing the same thing. People whispered it was the result of witchcraft.

New Englanders were largely Puritan. They were sober folk who forbade singing, dancing, holidays, and playing with toys, but that was nothing in comparison to their horror of witchcraft. There had been rumours of it in nearby villages, and it was quickly decided that the girls' afflictions were caused by evil worshipers of Satan.

Possible suspects were rounded up: a homeless beggar, a neighbour the girls' family had been arguing with, and a black or Indian slave.

Things swiftly escalated, and more women were arrested, including one who had been al about the girls' behaviour. Unlike the first batch, these people included upstanding, churchgoing members of the community – and if *they* could be witches, anyone could!

As the hysteria spread around the colony, men as well as women were charged. Even a four-year-old was interrogated. Her answers were used to implicate her mother.

Twenty people were hanged from a tree in Salem; the cart that brought them was used as the scaffold. Another four died in jail. A hundred more were released from prison when severe frost hit the county, and the panic subsided – but the damage had been done. Families had accused families, friends had pointed fingers at friends, and innocent people had died.

Recently, some people have claimed the hysteria experienced by the women in the New England witch trials might have been caused by a rare, mosquito-borne epidemic, not unlike a strange sleeping disease that occurred in the early twentieth century, which saw patients behaving in similar ways.

The townsfolk experienced strange fits, resulting in whispers of witchcraft.

25

Evidence

Investigators breaking into a suspected witch's home might find all kinds of "evidence". The kitchen table probably also did serve as a devil-worshiping altar, and that knife she'd been using to chop cabbage was highly suspicious. The cooking pot was almost certainly the witch's cauldron, and there was no way the doll left behind by her grandchild was a toy. It was clearly a "poppet" – a model of someone she wanted to harm. She would stab it with a pin, and the person would die!

The stick and rope in the corner were her wand and magical binding cords – and what could she possibly want with a broomstick other than as a mode of transport? Admittedly, if they found a magic circle chalked onto the floor, it was less easy to explain, but that rarely happened.

In case the "witch" tried to speak in her defence, or worse, utter evil spells, she was occasionally forced to wear a "witches' bridle", sometimes called "branks" or a "scold's bridle", as it was also used for nagging wives or people who committed slander. The nasty metal contraption clamped around the head, so the victim couldn't speak. Branks were particularly popular in Scotland.

A woman forced to wear a "Witches' Bridle".

Pricking Needles

The accused would be stripped and examined for moles, scars, birthmarks, or skin imperfections. Since most people have at least one or two moles, the examiners usually found something.

If they were "witches' marks", these imperfections wouldn't bleed or feel pain when they were pricked with a needle. We now know some professional "witch-prickers" were actually con-artists. Several of their "special needles" have survived to modern times and reveal a shocking secret: they had retractable points!

If the pricker wanted to find someone innocent, they'd give them a good jab with the full needle. The accused would shout "Ouch!" and be sent home innocent.

If the pricker wanted to find them guilty (perhaps they hadn't paid a large enough bribe!), they'd retract the needle into its handle as they "pierced" the skin. The person would, of course, neither bleed nor feel any pain – until they were executed!

Witches' Garments

Imagine a witch today, and two main things usually come to mind: a pointy hat and a big black cloak. Back in the seventeenth century, though, that's what a lot of people used to wear! If you look at woodcuts of the Salem trials, for example, both men and women are wearing conical hats and cloaks.

Once upon a time, conical hats were considered rather scandalous. When they first came into fashion (think of medieval damsels with pointed headdresses and wafty veils), church men were very suspicious. The bishop of Paris claimed they represented the horns of the devil!

Familiars

If you ticked the "lonely old lady" box, heaven help you if you also had a pet. Everyone knew witches kept animal servants, or "familiars". They were actually evil imps who could change shape when they liked. They might choose to look like dogs, cats, mice, rats, roosters – you name it – and they might look cuddly, but underneath they were demons, in league with Satan himself.

Court accounts name a highly suspicious greyhound named Vinegar Tom, a toad named Pigin, and a lamb named Tiffin. Especially suspect was Jamara, a fat spaniel, and other familiars such as Pyewhacket and Grizzel Greedigut were not to be trusted. Matthew Hopkins announced even their names could not have been invented by a mortal! They lived on human blood, supplied by the witch herself.

Witch Bottles

People were so scared of witchcraft that they even built magic charms against it into their houses. "Witch bottles" were jars filled with nasty stuff and buried under the entrance to homes. They were designed to give witches terrible pain if they crossed the threshold.

Witch bottles were often Bellarmine jugs in the shape of strange, bearded faces. One was recently found in Greenwich, England, still sealed with its contents. X-rays show it contained eight bent pins, ten nail clippings, a leather heart with a nail through it, belly-button fluff, and human urine! Chances are that concoction kept more than witches away...

Celebrity Memoirs

Just like famous people today, witchfinders cashed in on their notoriety by publishing books. Full of explicit, gruesome details about the "horrors of sorcery", they were bestsellers.

King James I's *Daemonologie* became a sort of witchfinder's handbook, though even the king later began to wonder if he'd been a bit harsh. John Stearne wrote *A Confirmation and Discovery of Witchcraft,* while Matthew Hopkins' diss-and-tell, *The Discovery of Witches,* revealed his methods, which frankly, were comprised of torture under the name of interrogation.

JULIUS CAESAR AND MARCUS JUNIUS BRUTUS

Et tu, Brute?

44 BCE

Word was getting around: Julius Caesar was getting a little too big for his sandals. However much the Roman statesman protested "I am Caesar, not king", no one believed him. He accepted titles such as "Dictator for Life" and "Father of the Fatherland" and had a golden throne at the Senate House. He rode around in a ceremonial chariot and rejigged the calendar, naming the seventh month after himself: July. Senators were convinced his next move would be to do away with their hard-won republic altogether.

Some of them started plotting against the egotistical leader, led by Gaius Cassius and Caesar's one-time friend Marcus Junius Brutus. They all agreed – the dictator needed to go for the sake of the republic, but how to do the dirty deed?

Maybe they could wait until the elections and push Caesar off his platform into the waiting daggers of accomplices? Hmmm, not bad, but the elections were a long way off. Perhaps he could be attacked by "thugs" along the Sacred Way, Rome's main street, or as he went to the theatre?

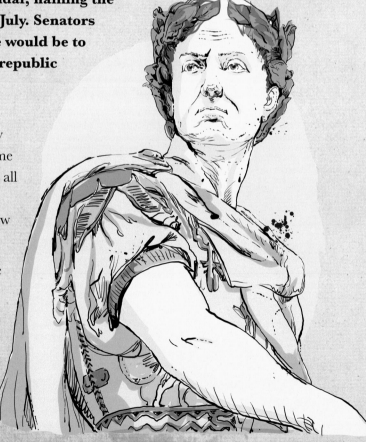

Julius Caesar was popular among the citizens of Rome, but not with the Senate.

Twenty-three stab wounds took Caesar's life.

Caesar provided the perfect opportunity himself. He called a Senate meeting on the Ides (15th) of March. Bingo!

A soothsayer, Spurinna, tried to warn Caesar it was a bad idea, and Julius had bad dreams, too. On the fateful day he woke up feeling poorly, but he was persuaded not to disappoint the Senate. As he arrived, Caesar was handed a note warning of his death, but he just added it to his pile of mail for reading later. He joked with Spurinna, saying, "The Ides of March are come".

"Aye Caesar", replied the soothsayer, "but not gone".

The senators came forward as if to say something. Then one of them, a man named Casca, slipped behind Caesar and stabbed him in the throat. Caesar grabbed Casca's arm, piercing it with his stylus (a sharp writing implement), but someone else had already plunged their own knife into him. Confronted by a sea of daggers, Caesar readjusted his toga to look as regal as possible and pulled his gown over his face.

Caesar's shredded body was carried back to his house in a litter, one arm hanging out of the side for the gawking crowds to see.

Julius Caesar

Julius Caesar was never officially the emperor, though he acted like one. He was a brilliant general and very popular with his own army. Ordinary citizens liked him too, for bringing in tax cuts, improving roads, and putting on free entertainment, though the people who were transported to other countries so he didn't have to give them free corn were less delighted. He was considered merciful to his enemies (by Roman standards, anyway!) and was a hit with the ladies – he even had a son with the Egyptian queen, Cleopatra. But the power was definitely going to his head. He even had a statue of himself paraded alongside the Roman gods around his amphitheatre at games!

Marcus Junius Brutus

Originally fighting for Pompey, one of Julius Caesar's rivals, Brutus was first captured, but he was then pardoned by Caesar, who had been fond of his mother. He trusted Brutus, who was very quickly made a high-ranking magistrate called a praetor. Brutus had initially thought Caesar's plans for the republic were a good idea, but he was shocked when Caesar started acting like he was a god.

Not that Brutus himself was an angel. He was arrogant, cruel, and very greedy. He once arranged a lift of a cap on interest rates so he could lend money at nearly 50 percent interest! He made sure payments kept rolling in by having city officials murdered.

The Ides of March

Caesar, like all Romans, was very superstitious. When he was a boy, a horse was born on his estate that had five toes. A soothsayer declared whoever could ride it would one day rule the world. The young Julius took the precaution of rearing it and riding it himself.

Spurinna was a special kind of soothsayer called a haruspex, who specialized in reading the "exta", or entrails, of sacrificed animals. A haruspex also interpreted bolts of lightning and other omens. He advised Caesar to beware the Ides of March. Caesar should have listened.

Forewarned but Not Forearmed

There were plenty of other warnings of the forthcoming assassination. A herd of horses stopped eating grass and started shedding tears. The day before the Ides a little bird called a king wren flew into the Pompeian Assembly Room with a sprig of laurel in its beak. It was followed by a swarm of other birds who tore it to pieces.

Some workmen accidentally dug up a tomb. Its tablet said: "Disturb the bones of Capys and a man of Trojan stock will be murdered by his kindred, later avenged at great cost".

It's hardly surprising both Caesar and his wife Calpurnia had terrible nightmares.

Laurel Wreaths

Caesar was a pretty nifty dresser. He wore fancy togas with wrist-length sleeves and fringes, shaved regularly, and kept the rest of his body smooth using tweezers, but he was going bald on top, which his enemies thought was hilarious. He grew the few strands of hair he did have really long and combed them over the top of his head. When the Senate granted him the privilege of wearing a laurel wreath, he did – all the time!

Caesar's comet rose for seven days.

Caesar's Comet

It was traditional to hold special gladiatorial games to honour the funerals of Roman celebrities. Julius Caesar's games were especially grand, but one spooky celestial "guest" gave everyone, especially the conspirators, the creeps.

In a peculiar twist of fate, one of the brightest comets ever recorded happened to coincide with the commemorations. It rose for seven successive days, and the superstitious Romans believed the "Star of Caesar" must be the dead man's soul come to haunt them – after all, Caesar had always claimed he was descended from the goddess Venus.

Modern astronomers studying the records of ancient Roman and Chinese stargazers believe Caesar's Comet would have been visible in daylight. The Great Comet was so important that it was even featured on coins.

Et Tu Brute?

William Shakespeare's play *Julius Caesar* has the dying commander say, "Et tu, Brute?" ("You too, Brutus?") as he sees his former friend about to plunge a dagger into his chest. Shakespeare got the idea from the Roman historian (and outrageous gossip!) Suetonius, who reported that others said Caesar actually spoke in Greek – "*Kai su teknon*?" meaning "You also, my child?" Whatever was really said, the meaning is the same: Julius felt betrayed by a man he had trusted.

Caesar's Funeral

When they heard of their leader's assassination, the ordinary citizens of Rome became crazed with grief and anger. Since it would take a long while to organize a formal funeral, everyone was allowed to do whatever they liked – and they did.

It started out reasonably enough. A herald read out a decree declaring Caesar a god, and Caesar's successor, Mark Antony, made a speech. Then things went off the rails.

There was an argument outside the Forum over where the new god should be cremated. As tempers flared, a couple of "divine forms" appeared and set fire to the body then and there. Everyone piled in, burning whatever was on hand – chairs, clothes, jewellery, anything.

A riot exploded across the city. One poor guy called Cinna, whom the mob mistook for another man with the same name who'd once made a speech against Caesar, was murdered; his head was then cut off and paraded around the streets on the end of a spear. The mob also tried to burn down the houses of Brutus and Cassius and were only stopped with difficulty.

THE GUNPOWDER PLOT

SEVENTEENTH CENTURY, ENGLAND

Remember, remember the Fifth of November! Gunpowder, treason, and plot ...

In the early hours of 5 November 1605, a suspicious-looking man in a cloak and hat was discovered hiding in the basement of the Houses of Parliament in Westminster, England. He had a pocket watch, a match – and thirty-six barrels of gunpowder.

Guy Fawkes was in charge of lighting the fuse.

After Queen Elizabeth I's death, any hopes Roman Catholics in England might have had that the new king would be more tolerant toward them were dashed. James I was even more fervent in his persecution of Catholics than Elizabeth had been.

One man, Robert Catesby, decided he'd had enough. He invited some friends to the Dog and Duck pub near the River Thames and told them his plan. Why not get rid of the king, his advisers, and Parliament all at once by blowing up the House of Lords? Maybe God even designed the place for their punishment!

Catesby and company rented the building's basement, filled it with gunpowder, and waited for the king to arrive for the grand State Opening of Parliament. At the last minute, however, someone wrote an anonymous letter that was handed to Robert Cecil, the king's spymaster. The plot was revealed, and Guy Fawkes, the man in charge of lighting the fuse, was caught red-handed.

The other conspirators fled to Holbeach House in the Midlands, where they tried to dry their soaked gunpowder in front of the fire. It was not the best idea. The whole lot exploded, burning, blinding, and maiming several of them.

The house was surrounded by the local militia. The rebels resolved to fight to the death, side by side. There are still holes in the walls from the final shoot-out. Robert Catesby was killed by the same musket ball as his friend Thomas Percy. Two more conspirators died; most of the rest were captured and dragged down to the Tower of London for trial along with Guy Fawkes.

They were found guilty of treason and sentenced to be hanged, drawn, and quartered. Guy Fawkes was lucky – he jumped off the scaffold and died before his innards were cut out and burned, but the rest were all disemboweled while they were still alive. Afterward, their heads were displayed on pikes on London Bridge so people would never forget the Fifth of November.

Guy Fawkes

Guy Fawkes converted to Catholicism when he was very young. When he was twenty-one, he travelled to Europe to join the Spanish Catholics who were fighting the Protestant Dutch. The dashing adventurer, with his flowing hair and bushy beard, was popular and loyal. His fellow soldiers nicknamed him "Guido", the Italian version of his name, and he was made a captain.

He tried to persuade the Spanish king, Philip, to support a possible rebellion against King James, but Philip said no, even though the two countries were technically still at war. Fawkes came home and was invited to join Catesby's gang.

As an explosives expert, Fawkes' job was to obtain the gunpowder and ignite it. He had a long fuse so that he could run away once it was lit, but he never actually got to make the fateful spark. The king's spymaster, Robert Cecil, was onto him.

People were tortured "on the rack".

Robert Cecil

Robert Cecil's dad, William, Lord Burghley, was Queen Elizabeth's most trusted adviser for most of her reign. He had built himself a very handy network of spies and a fearsome secret police, which Robert inherited when he began to serve King James. When the queen died, Cecil arrested "known troublemakers", including Robert Catesby, to make sure James would take the throne easily. He encouraged the new king to reintroduce harsh laws against Catholics. James was delighted at Cecil's loyalty, calling him "my little elf", but Catesby was furious and even more determined to bring down the king.

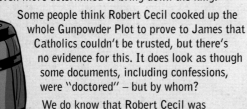

Some people think Robert Cecil cooked up the whole Gunpowder Plot to prove to James that Catholics couldn't be trusted, but there's no evidence for this. It does look as though some documents, including confessions, were "doctored" – but by whom?

We do know that Robert Cecil was instrumental in uncovering the conspiracy and making absolutely sure the traitors were silenced for good.

Torture

Down in the interrogation cells, Guy Fawkes wasn't playing ball. His captors were frustrated, but secretly impressed at his stubbornness and wit. When they asked him why he'd taken a trip to Flanders, he said it was to pass the time. The only name he revealed was the fellow whose vault he'd been caught in, which they knew anyway.

At first the "gentler tortures" were tried, but the king told them to keep going until "the ultimate is reached". Fawkes was most likely put on the rack, but whatever torture was used, it broke him. When he finally signed his confession, he could hardly write.

An Anonymous Letter

On 26 October 1605, a tall stranger, his features concealed by the night, left a letter for William Parker, Lord Monteagle. Parker, who was eating supper, got a servant to read the letter aloud. It contained a warning: there would be an explosion at the opening of Parliament, and he should make sure he wasn't around when the big bang happened. He was instructed to burn the letter after reading it.

Parker went straight to the king, and the plot was discovered. To this day nobody one knows who sent the letter. It was unsigned, and no one, even under torture, claimed it was them, even though it might have helped their cause. Some people think it was written by the king's men to try to catch the conspirators.

An Unusual Use for Orange Juice

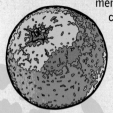

Several Jesuit priests were suspected of being involved in the intrigue. One of the most wanted men, Father Henry Garnet, communicated via letters with secret messages written in invisible ink made from orange juice. He was captured and suffered the same fate as everyone else.

Priest Holes

Ever since Elizabethan times, illegal Jesuit priests had hidden from the authorities in tiny, dark spaces concealed in the homes of wealthy Catholics. Under stairs, between walls, and in roof spaces, these "hides" were so cunningly constructed that some of them are only being discovered today.

The best priest-hole builder was Nicholas Owen, who worked for Henry Garnet and spent eighteen years constructing mysterious miniature masterpieces all over the country. Owen eventually gave himself up to the priest hunters to distract attention from where his master was hiding. He was tortured to death for his efforts, but his extraordinary work can still be seen in many country houses.

Fireworks

The night the Papist Plot was foiled, bells rang out and bonfires were lit to celebrate the king's lucky escape. Ever since, "Guy Fawkes Night" has seen bonfires, fireworks, celebration, and general rowdiness on the streets. Children used to make their own stuffed figures out of old clothes stuffed with newspaper, asking neighbours for "a penny for the guy".

Some towns, such as Lewes in Sussex, England, spend the whole year preparing for the event, making giant effigies of Guy Fawkes, as well as Pope Paul V – who, in 1605, was the hated head of the Catholic Church – and various modern-day "enemies". People stuff the figures with fireworks so they explode on bonfires after parading around the streets with them dressed as smugglers and throwing firecrackers by the light of burning torches.

Even today, before the State Opening of Parliament, the Yeomen of the Guard still search the cellars at the Palace of Westminster, just in case…

Puppet Princess

Who was going to rule when the king and all his politicians were dead? The plotters decided to crown a "puppet" monarch, so they could secretly rule behind the scenes.

By "innocently chatting" with servants, they realized young Prince Charles was heavily guarded. Besides, the staircase they were going to sneak up to snatch him had been blocked off. They couldn't figure out how to get to seven-month-old Princess Mary either, but her older sister, Princess Elizabeth, was fair game and living in the countryside.

Handsome, charming Sir Everard Digby set off with his dogs, trunks full of money, and pretty clothes, pretending to be on a hunting party. The plan was to persuade nine-year-old Elizabeth to join him, and then to kidnap her, but Digby was caught before he could do the deed.

Some towns make giant effigies of Guy Fawkes.

LA MALINCHE

> *"After God we owe this conquest of New Spain to Doña Marina". — Hernán Cortés*

Aztec emperor Moctezuma II was convinced he was the most powerful ruler in all of what is now Mexico. When news arrived of strangers from across the sea, Moctezuma was suspicious. He was already getting bad omens. A temple roof had burned, a ghost had been heard wailing mournfully, a lake had boiled, and a comet appeared in the heavens that not even his priests could explain. On top of everything, it was the end of a fifty-two-year cycle in the Aztec calendar, and everyone knew nothing good happened then.

When Moctezuma actually met Spanish conquistador Hernán Cortés, the two men warily exchanged gifts. Moctezuma's present went over a little too well. Cortés' eyes lit up at the sight of so much gold. He had come for power and wealth, as well as to convert these human-sacrificing cannibals to Christianity. This was his opportunity.

Cortés' best hope was to divide and rule. He wanted to ally with the chiefs of territories whom Moctezuma had conquered and humiliated, but he had a problem: he couldn't speak Nahuatl, the Aztec language. He'd rescued a shipwrecked priest a few years back who had been translating for him, but he only understood Mayan.

Hernán Cortés and Moctezuma exchanged gifts.

Then someone told Cortés a slave he'd been given could speak "Mexican", and a teenage girl named Malinalli was brought before him. She translated Nahuatl into Mayan, and the priest could then translate Mayan into Spanish. It was a long process, but Cortés was impressed.

Malinalli was converted to Christianity, and "Doña Marina" became the conquistador's translator, adviser, secretary, and eventually, his lover. "La Malinche", as she was known by the Aztecs, is shown in illustrations at Cortés' side and even sometimes on her own during negotiations with chiefs, princes, and ambassadors, helping to create alliances and plan battles.

Moctezuma was taken prisoner and then killed, with each side blaming the other for his death. After a fierce, bloody war, the Aztecs were defeated.

La Malinche didn't just translate words. She interpreted two cultures, trying to explain the vast differences between European and Aztec customs, but this didn't make her popular with her own people. She has been considered a traitor to Mexico ever since.

Hernán Cortés persuaded Diego Velázquez de Cuéllar to let him command his own fleet.

La Malinche

Malinalli, named for the goddess of grass, was born into a noble family sometime between 1496 and 1501. Later she was also called Tenepal, or "one who speaks with liveliness". That skill was going to be useful…

When Malinalli's father died, her mother married another chieftain, and they had a son. Malinalli was now a potential threat to the young prince, so she was sold to passing slave traders, from whom she learned Mayan. That would come in handy, too…

When Malinalli was given to Cortés with nineteen other slave women, her linguistic skills made her useful. When she learned Spanish, she became indispensable.

Both sides depended on La Malinche's accuracy, and she held a lot of power – she decided when and what to translate. When she learned of a plan by the people of Cholula to help the Aztecs attack the Spanish, she pretended to play along – informing Cortés of their every move. Instead of mounting an ambush, the Cholulans were themselves massacred in their own city plaza.

Doña Marina and Hernan Cortés had a son. Some consider Martín Cortés, with European and Aztec parents, as the first recorded Mexican.

Hernán Cortés

Hernán Cortés was born in 1485 in western Spain. He studied law, but found it boring, so he became a swashbuckling seafarer instead. Sailing with the famous conquistador Diego Velázquez de Cuéllar, he helped his commander conquer Cuba, but Cortés wanted more.

He had heard of great wealth in a newly discovered land to the south and persuaded Velázquez to let him command his own fleet. Velázquez had a last-minute change of heart and said no, but Cortés ignored him and set sail anyway.

Cortés set about invading what is now Mexico, wiping out the indigenous population with efficient cruelty and building new colonies in what he called New Spain.

At home, the Spanish started to worry that Cortés was becoming too powerful. He was called back home, but he went adventuring again, this time discovering California.

Quetzalcoatl

Legend tells that when a mountain was seen moving on the sea, the Aztecs thought it was the prophesized return of the plumed serpent god of the wind, Quetzalcoatl. The "mountain" was actually a Spanish ship, and "Quetzalcoatl" was the Spanish invader Cortés. But divine invader or not, Moctezuma was left with a dilemma: What happens to a king when a god comes along to take his place?

Since the story only began in the 1530s, it may have been Spanish propaganda invented to make the Aztecs look gullible.

Blood Sacrifice

The Spanish were horrified by the Aztec practise of human sacrifice, despite their own use of eye-popping torture and hideous execution methods.

The Aztecs, though, weren't "punishing" victims; they were "giving" them to the gods, offering the most precious thing they had: blood. It was an honour to be a sacrifice – you'd be dressed in fine clothes, jewels, and feathers, and people would kiss the flower-strewn ground you walked upon.

The towering steps of the Great Temple ran with the blood of many thousands of victims, their still-beating hearts ripped out by priests and held aloft for the gods. The hearts were ritually burned and the bodies thrown down the temple steps.

One Spanish priest watched a man being sacrificed. One of his thighs was sent down for Moctezuma's dinner; the rest was divided up among other nobles and served with maize. By eating parts of another human, Aztecs believed they were achieving a true communion with each other, but the Spanish weren't hungry.

Human sacrifice was a serious handicap to the Aztecs. Killing their own people depleted stocks of warriors; killing their neighbours bred enemies. In battle they were unwilling to kill the Spanish, as they wanted to sacrifice them later, but they couldn't control their prisoners and were overwhelmed.

It was an honour to be an Aztec sacrifice to the gods.

The Silent Killer

Even if Cortés' weapons didn't kill the Aztecs, European diseases would have done the trick. One of Cortés' soldiers contracted smallpox from a slave on another ship. The Aztecs attacked Cortés' army, and the soldier was killed.

Looters searching his body got more than they bargained for. The Aztecs had no immunity to smallpox, and thousands died, including the new emperor Cuitláhuac. When entire families died, their houses were just pulled down over them.

Gold Fever

The Spanish may not have enjoyed the bloodletting, but they were partial to some of the Aztecs' treasure. They liked the spices and the slaves, the cacao and tobacco, but they *loved* the gold.

Oddly, the Aztecs weren't that obsessed with gold, except when it was made into works of art to please the gods. They called it *teocuitlatl*, from the words "god" or "divine" and "excrement" – so gold was literally "god-poop". Other precious metals and stones, like silver, turquoise, and jet, were differently coloured excrement, though "excrement" could also sometimes mean "snot", "earwax", or other bodily goop. Whichever god-excrement it was, it was pretty enough for jewellery but too soft to be useful as weapons, so they rated other things, like exotic feathers, crystal, and even pitchstone, more highly.

Some say Moctezuma lost his empire the moment he handed over those golden goodies on that first meeting. The Spanish were mesmerized by the sight of the Aztec emperor's royal coffers and demanded more and more gold, and when given beautifully worked objects, the Spanish melted them down for the base metal.

Even when their lives were at risk, some retreating Spanish soldiers were drowned, weighed down by all their gold.

Some Spanish soldiers drowned, weighed down by their gold.

La Malinche Today

Over the centuries, Mexican people have struggled to understand why La Malinche would "betray" her people to the Spanish. Many still see her as the embodiment of treachery. Even the word *malinchista* means someone who is disloyal to their country, especially in Mexico.

More recently, however, people have started looking at her in different ways.

Some see her as a victim, saying she was sold into slavery and, given a situation she didn't choose, made the best decisions she could. They argue she saved thousands of lives by negotiation rather than slaughter and even helped to stop the tradition of human sacrifice.

Others see her as the mother of the modern Mexican people, a bridge between Europeans and Native Mesoamerican Indians.

The Aztec Calendar

The Aztecs believed time consisted of a chain of fifty-two-year cycles. When the chain was complete, the world would end. At the end of each cycle, the cosmos became misaligned, and bad things happened. It might even be the end of the world. So a special sacrifice was performed to welcome the sun on the dawn of each new cycle and to prevent the Tzitzimime, or twilight monsters, from attacking the living. Priests would watch for the constellation Pleiades from the Hill of the Star, and then they would light a fire in the hollow chest of a sacrificed victim. From it, runners would ignite torches and relight all the altars and hearths in the city.

TURNCOATS AND SPIES

Some of the most hated people in history are those who turned their back on their country, their friends, or their beliefs. However bad they may have been, they usually had their reasons. We often just don't know them...

Benedict Arnold

When George Washington turned up at the garrison of West Point on the Hudson, he was expecting to be greeted by a legendary Patriot general. Benedict Arnold had helped capture Fort Ticonderoga and invade Canada. He was a hero, wasn't he?

But Arnold wasn't home. He had apparently cleared out in a big hurry after hearing a British spy had been captured. Washington was still puzzled the next day until he saw what the spy had been carrying: letters in Arnold's handwriting giving away details of the defences at West Point. America's hero had turned his coat and was now batting for the British.

Ever since, people have wondered why such an enthusiastic supporter of independence betrayed his fellow rebels. The truth is, we'll never really know.

Mata Hari

Margaretha Geertruida MacLeod, better known as, "Mata Hari", started performing as an exotic dancer in Paris in 1905. Her racy costumes and "Far Eastern" dances weren't very authentic, but no one minded. She was a big hit and particularly popular with army officers.

This put her in the perfect position to become a spy, but it's unclear just who she was spying for – if anyone at all! The Germans offered her money for French information, and the French asked her to spy for *them*. What actually went on is still obscure today. This didn't stop the French from imprisoning, trying, and sentencing her to death by firing squad in 1917. (The papers about her case, which may reveal more, were declared secret for one hundred years. They are due to be released in 2017.)

Sir Faithful Fortescue

Probably the least well-named general in the English Civil War, Sir Faithful Fortescue was anything but faithful.

Just before the battle of Edgehill, Sir Fortescue, who was commanding a troop of cavalry for the Parliamentarians, switched sides to fight for the king instead.

There was just one problem: many of his men forgot to take off their orange "Roundhead" sashes and were attacked by the army they had just joined!

Casanova

Giacomo Casanova is best known today as a bold adventurer and a huge hit with the ladies, but according to his diaries, he was much more. Church man, musician, diplomat, soldier, writer – and the man who introduced the lottery to Paris – Casanova was also a master spy.

Stuck inside an "inescapable prison" in Venice for being a "magician", he made a spectacular jailbreak, and then he roamed Europe, charming everyone wherever he went – except, of course, the fellow he challenged to a duel!

Back in Rome, the Vatican realized how useful this prancing peacock could be and offered him a job as a spy. Spies were usually silent and watchful. No one would suspect anyone as colourful, noisy, and indiscreet as Casanova!

William Hare

William Hare and William Burke were best friends. They were also the most notorious body snatchers in Scotland, digging up dead people to sell to medical schools. They soon got bored with the effort of digging and started supplying corpses to order in Edinburgh's dark and foggy streets. Since people didn't generally *die* to order, a little murder became necessary.

Need to dissect a young woman? Certainly, sir. An old man? No problem, we have one *just in.* A small boy? Amazingly, we actually have one dying as you speak…

The city lived in fear, and the authorities closed in. Burke and Hare were captured after someone found a dead body stuffed under Burke's bed. Neither confessed, but on being promised his freedom, Hare "turned King's evidence" and sold his friend down the river. It was all Burke's idea. *He'd* done all the killing. Poor William Hare was *entirely innocent.* Honest.

William Burke was hanged on 28 January 1829, and publicly dissected, just like his victims. William Hare was released a few days later and left town right away. He was sighted south of the border, and then he was never seen again.

Belle Boyd

There were many spies on both sides in the American Civil War, but few of them took the form of a genteel young lady who'd shot a man dead for insulting her mother. Isabella Boyd was put under house arrest, where she sweet-talked one of the officers into revealing secrets.

Belle was fearless, hiding in cupboards, listening through knotholes, sending secret messages, and falsifying papers. She even rode through enemy fire to relay some information to General Stonewall Jackson and had a skirt full of bullet holes to prove it. Boyd was caught no fewer than three times, but each time she managed to get herself released.

TRIALS, TORTURE, AND EXECUTION

Animal Trials

Today we would think it crazy to sue a dog, cat, parrot, or donkey. But in the Middle Ages, animals were held accountable for their actions, just like humans, and they were tried and usually found guilty. After all, they didn't have much to say for themselves in court!

Trials were taken very seriously. Lawyers were called, often paid for by the town, and evidence was heard on both sides. Deliberation was as sober as for any human. Sometimes the animals were acquitted; more often they were found guilty and executed as an example to other animals that might be tempted to commit crimes.

In 1266, a pig was found guilty of murdering a child.

The first recorded trial was of a pig in 1266, in France, who was found guilty of murdering and eating a child. On another occasion a whole herd was convicted. Only three of the pigs had actually trampled the swineherd's son to death, but the rest had heard the commotion, rushed over to watch, and grunted encouragement to the three homicidal hogs.

Cows, goats, sparrows, and even snails all felt the long arm of the law. While murder or theft was tried in criminal courts, beasts accused of "public nuisance" offenses were called before the ecclesiastical or church courts. Individual critters were summoned to represent the "group" in a sort of class action. A rat might represent all its friends who had been accused of bringing plague to a village, or a caterpillar would be commanded to answer for a swarm that had destroyed a crop. The entire group would be sentenced together, usually ordered to leave town by a specific date.

When they failed to do so (which amazingly, happened quite often), excuses were made – the flies hadn't all heard the expulsion order, or the rats were scared of the cats in town and were lying low.

However crazy we may find the practise, it was just another way medieval people tried to understand what was happening in their world. Science was in its infancy, and for them anything bad that happened was usually because someone – or something – had offended God. Not knowing about germs and viruses, people assumed the animals had either been sent by God as a punishment or were deliberately harming humans.

Hue and Cry

In early English times, if someone had witnessed a criminal act or had been wronged, they were expected to raise the "hue and cry" – to shout for help. At this point, all able-bodied men were obliged to chase and arrest the accused person, even if they turned out to be innocent. Indeed, if the neighbours didn't join in and the suspect got away, they could be liable for any damage the victim had suffered.

If the suspect had evidence on them – perhaps they still held the murder weapon or had a swag bag of stolen goodies – or if they resisted capture, they could be killed on the spot. If they didn't resist, they'd be taken to court.

The fugitive could always slip into the local church and claim sanctuary. Sometimes they just had to get to the church before their pursuers; other times they had to ring a special bell, rap on a "sanctuary" door knocker, or sit on a "frith stool". They then had forty days of immunity before either giving themselves up or confessing their guilt and going into permanent exile. A popular third option was to wait until the guards fell asleep and run away!

A "Sanctuary" door knocker.

Pleading the Belly

As far back as 1387, one way a woman could avoid being executed was to tell the judge she was expecting a baby. If the mother was hanged, her unborn baby would die too, and then the court would be guilty of killing an innocent person because the child had committed no crime. It was a popular plea and saved many women, as afterward their sentences were often commuted to imprisonment, transportation, or even pardons so that they could care for their child.

Of course some women said they were pregnant just so they could get out of being hanged, but they tended to be found out!

Two of the most famous women to "plead their bellies" were the dread pirates Mary Read and Anne Bonny. Mary Read died in prison, but we don't know what happened to Anne Bonny – perhaps she even got away with it!

TORTURE

To inflict severe pain on someone, usually to force them to do or say something.

It's almost unfathomable what humans think of to inflict on other humans. The most inventive tortures were arguably created during medieval times, but all eras come up with acts of utmost cruelty. Don't try these at home, folks...

The Rack

Doesn't sound so bad, does it – being strapped to a device that slowly stretches your limbs? After all, stretching is good for you, isn't it?

Try being stretched so much that your arms and legs leave their sockets with an audible "pop". Going to confess now? No? Then your body is clearly ready to be stretched some more. How about pulling your limbs so much that they're literally torn from your body (slowly, too)? Could be your arms, could be your legs...want to bet on which goes first?

The rack was in use for hundreds of years, ranging from early, crude devices to industrial-level machinery, using rollers, handles, ratchets, and pulleys. Other tortures might be used at the same time, such as pulling out fingernails with red-hot pincers or burning the flesh with torches.

The next prisoner in line would often be shown the previous victim being racked. It was usually enough to loosen their tongues.

Heretic's Fork

The Heretic's Fork

Simple but effective, this small device was a double-ended fork attached to a collar. One end was placed under the victim's chin, the other rested on his breastbone. The victim was then suspended from the ceiling so he couldn't lie down.

At first it didn't seem too bad – the victim's muscles held up his head, though he could hardly speak. As the hours went on, however, the prisoner became more and more exhausted. He desperately wanted to relax his head, but the forks began to pierce his throat and chest. Unable to sleep, he knew if he nodded off for even a moment, he'd spear himself.

A similar torture was equally simple: a collar with iron spikes all the way around it. The victim couldn't lie down, move, or sleep for days on end if he didn't want to send a series of iron nails through his gullet.

Pillory or Stocks

Pillories and stocks were very similar. The pillory tended to have holes in it for the head and hands; the stocks secured your feet. They were often fixtures in a town marketplace.

The stocks were intended to inflict public humiliation rather than severe pain, though being pelted by your fellow villagers was often painful, depending on what was being thrown. If it was rotten vegetables, dead animals, or excrement, it was just revolting. If it was old boots, stones, or bricks, it could be fatal.

The famous author Daniel Defoe, who wrote *Robinson Crusoe*, was put in the stocks for penning a rude pamphlet about the way the Church treated people who didn't conform. Instead of chucking rotten eggs, the crowd threw flowers.

People were put in the stocks to be publicly humiliated.

Iron Maiden

The Iron Maiden was the opposite of the rack – instead of stretching, the victim was compressed, locked in an iron cabinet with spikes inside. The spikes weren't long enough to immediately kill the victim, just impale, though the ones cunningly devised to go through the eyeballs would have pretty much ensured blindness.

No one's actually sure if the Iron Maiden (so called because one found in Nuremberg had a woman's head as a sick decoration) was ever actually used. It might be a ghoulish fake, used for exhibitions, albeit based on a similar device called a *schandmantel,* or "coat of shame".

The schandmantel consisted of a barrel that people were forced to wear, almost like a portable pillory. Allegedly it also occasionally had spikes inside.

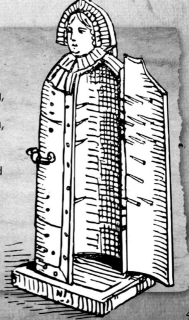

EXECUTION METHODS

Fifteen men on a dead man's chest...

Hanging

Hanging was, until recently, one of the most common forms of execution in many countries. Hangings were often public and could be quite an occasion, drawing crowds to jeer – or cheer, depending on the criminal. There was a carnival atmosphere, with food and drink, and ballad-sheet sellers vying to be the first to print the prisoner's last speech. The word *gala* comes from "Gala Day", or more grimly, "Gallows Day".

Mass executions were common. In 1649, the "Triple Tree" at Tyburn hanged twenty-four prisoners at once: twenty-three men and one woman, convicted of burglary. Eventually, the prisoner was allowed the privacy of a hood in order to spare the public the sight of their last excruciating minutes.

Sometimes "minutes" was exactly that. If the hangman got it wrong (or right!), the convict would dangle in agony for ages before dying. Eventually, in 1886, Lord Aberdare created a "drop table" – a chart that, according to the prisoner's weight and height, recommended the length of rope to give a good, solid, and fairly quick kill, without actually decapitating the victim.

People would sometimes buy "ballad sheets" from hawkers at executions.

Hanging, Drawing, and Quartering

Agreed by many to be one of the most sadistic forms of execution of all time, "hanging, drawing, and quartering" should actually be "drawing, hanging, and quartering", though it's unlikely its victims would care about word order...

The "drawing" part was where the victim was strapped to a "hurdle", a bit like a fence panel, and dragged or "drawn" by horse to the gallows. There he was hanged by a short rope so he didn't die. He was cut down, parts of his body were hacked off, and his intestines were ripped out from his stomach. His innards were burned before his eyes – if he could actually see by this point. Then his head was cut off and his body divided into four quarters, sent to different places to be put on public display.

This extreme form of execution was originally devised for the pirate William Maurice in 1241, and it was usually used to punish treason. It was a punishment reserved for men; women were "merely" burned at the stake, for public decency!

Burning at the Stake

Traditionally, there were three methods for this most horrid method of execution. The best was to be strangled first, so the burning was merely symbolic. "Second best" was being tied up right inside with the wood piled all around you. You still got burned to death, but it was comparatively quick, as it was so hot.

Most sadistic of all was the one you usually see in woodcuts, where the victim was tied to a stake with the fire around their feet. Artists loved how dramatic it looked, but it was absolute torture for the victim as the fire started around their feet and the flames slowly licked upward. The best they could hope for was to be overcome by the smoke.

Sicilian Bull

The "Brazen Bull" was said to have been created in ancient Greece by an inventor from Athens named Perillos. A life-size bull cast in bronze, it was hollow with a door in the side, into which the victim was shoved. A fire was lit under the bull, and as the prisoner died, his screams wafted out of the bull's mouth so it looked like it was bellowing.

Legend has it that the tyrant Phalaris, who'd commissioned it, ordered Perillos to get inside and demonstrate, but once inside, Phalaris lit the fire. Perillos was eventually pulled out before he actually died, but instead of being rewarded, he was thrown from a mountain.

The legend also says, however, that Phalaris himself suffered death-by-bull when he was overthrown by an invader.

Guillotine

Incredibly, "Madame Guillotine", or "the national razor", was invented out of "kindness". Given the number of bungled executions – snapped hanging ropes, missed axe swings, and incomplete beheadings – a machine that would chop off the victim's head quickly and cleanly the first time was seen to be a blessing.

The prototype needed a few improvements. Some say it was Louis XVI who suggested an angled blade instead of a straight one that sometimes merely crushed the neck or even jammed. "Such a blade would be able to accommodate all necks", he reportedly announced. Nine months later, one of those necks was his own. Its ease of use was arguably one of the reasons the French Revolution was so very bloody.

Women sat knitting beside the guillotine during a public execution. They were nicknamed, "Tricoteuse".

Dissection

Scientific advances meant the medical profession needed more and more corpses. Anatomists needed to learn how the body worked, doctors had to perform operations, and in a time before anesthetic, surgeons tried to amputate limbs as quickly as possible.

No one, however, wanted *their* body cut up.

In 1751, an act was passed by the British Parliament, saying the corpses of executed murderers must be used for dissection (if they weren't tarred and gibbeted for public view, of course). It went some way to providing the medical schools with corpses, but was still inadequate.

"Resurrection Men" took to robbing graves for bodies. Some even turned to murder in their hunt for suitable cadavers. If they were caught, they helped supply the anatomists in a very personal way!

SHAH JAHAN
(REIGNED 1627–1658)

Blood's thicker than water, or so they say, but it's just as easily spilled if you're part of one of the most dysfunctional families in seventeenth-century India.

The dynasty's founder, the great Babur, studied his enemies' tactics and then bettered them, beating the Turkish, Afghan, and Persian armies to take what is now northern India.

Babur's grandson Akbar shrewdly married a princess from his biggest rivals, the Rajputs, and even more cleverly, brought non-Muslims, such as Hindus, Jains, and Buddhists, onto his side by stopping the "Jazia" – extra taxes they'd had to pay for not being Muslim – and involving them in government. A sage prophesized he'd have three sons, and he was so delighted when he did that he built the extraordinary city of Fatehpur Sikri on the spot where it had been foretold. He might not have been so keen to build if he'd had a crystal ball, though…

Jahangir, Akbar's son, started the trend of Mughal sons rebelling against their fathers. Bored with waiting to become emperor himself, he organized a revolt while his father was away fighting a war in the south. He was defeated, but he became emperor anyway when Akbar finally died.

Mughal Empire

Many of the things we imagine when we think of India's golden age happened during the rule of the Mughal dynasty. Some of the country's most famous landmarks were built then, and much of the exquisite art we associate with ancient India comes from that time.

Six of India's greatest emperors ruled over nearly 200 years in glittering splendour, luxurious living (by the rich!), and outrageous pleasure. They were times of great wealth, artistic beauty, and grandeur – but they were anything but peaceful.

Jahangir presided over a time of plenty, splashing cash on palace-building and opulence beyond imagination. He had more than twenty wives and consorts, including his favourite, Nur Jahan, "Light of the World". He also had a drinking habit, and he loved opium almost as much.

Jahangir was tolerant of other religions and encouraged debate between different faiths. He wasn't so tolerant of his own son leading an army against him. He had his oldest son blinded for leading a rebellion, but it didn't stop the court intrigues, brother fighting brother, cousin fighting cousin.

At the centre of it all was the ambitious Prince Khurram, later known as Emperor Shah Jahan.

Shah Jahan

Third son to Jahangir, young Prince Khurram was easily his father's favourite. Jahangir even weighed his son against gold, giving the money away as alms to the poor.

While still prince, Khurram subjugated the region of Udaipur, but he cleverly made the terms favourable enough to keep the people on his side. When Jahangir became ill, Prince Khurram fell out with his stepmother, Nur Jahan, who had become more and more powerful at court. For the last few years of Jahangir's life, Khurram was in open revolt against his father.

Shah Jahan and his wife, Mumtaz Mahal.

Khurram had a simple philosophy for ascending the throne: he just executed any male relatives he thought might be in the way. The technique was not lost on his sons.

As "Shah Jahan", Khurram governed for around thirty years, more or less in peace – from wars, that is. He expanded the empire and built a walled city, now Old Delhi, including the extraordinary Red Fort, which housed a legendary throne encrusted with gemstones and decorated with peacocks.

In 1657, Shah Jahan fell seriously ill, and the fight for succession began. Of his four sons, only two had much hope, but they all tried seizing the crown. The aging emperor recovered, but by now events had turned against him.

Aurangzeb

Dara Shikoh, Shah Jahan's oldest son, was the emperor's choice as successor. It's argued he may have continued the religious tolerance and love of the arts of his ancestors, but he didn't count on his younger brother Aurangzeb.

A cool, battle-hardened general, Aurangzeb hated Dara. He defeated the court-soft prince and had him executed. He also killed another brother and chased the fourth out of the country, where he died anyway. Aurangzeb wasn't letting go of power now that he had it, either. He made sure his father, Shah Jahan, was incarcerated in his own palace at Agra for eight years, until his death.

Aurangzeb was the opposite of his forebears. He lived an austere life, with religion at its centre. While his ancestors had loved pleasure, music, art, and debating religion, Aurangzeb's orthodox Muslim views frowned on any decoration that wasn't calligraphy, and he certainly didn't want to talk about other people's opinions. Artists and philosophers left to join the courts of neighbouring dynasties, such as the powerful Rajputs, with whom Aurangzeb went to war. He also picked fights with the Marathas, building a massive army where his predecessors had built bridges.

Powerful Women

Education for both sexes was important in Mughal India, and women held powerful positions within the royal household, albeit as wives rather than paid advisers.

Ruqaiya Sultana Begum, the first wife of the Emperor Akbar, could speak several languages, and although she didn't have any children herself, she raised the young Prince Khurram as her own.

Jahangir's wife, Nur Jahan, was well versed in music, poetry, literature, and dance. She was also a mean shot – it's said she once shot four tigers with six bullets. She was clever, too – when she and her husband were captured by rebels, she was the one who worked out the escape plan.

Nur Jahan, Shah Jahan's stepmother, was an incredible shot.

As Jahangir became ill, Nur Jahan took on more and more state business, even minting coins with her name on them. She introduced Prince Khurram to her niece, Mumtaz Mahal, who would become the love of his life, but he didn't thank her for it. Eventually he and his stepmother fell out.

Taj Mahal

When Shah Jahan's wife, Mumtaz Mahal, died suddenly after giving birth to her fourteenth child, the emperor was inconsolable. He spent two years in mourning, eventually deciding to create a magnificent tomb for her. It was to be the most beautiful building the world had ever known, a monument to their love.

He spent a long time looking at plans before deciding on a white marble fantasy of turrets, domes, minarets, and precious jewels, set in a water garden to reflect Shah Jahan's dream palace.

Legend says he planned to create a mirror image in black marble for himself on the opposite bank of the river Yamuna.

We will never know whether the story is true, as he was imprisoned before he could begin. We will also never know if Aurangzeb's decision to incarcerate his father so he could see – but not get to – his wife's memorial was an act of supreme kindness or cruelty.

Would You Like a Side Salad With That, Sir?

Aurangzeb was always jealous of the influence that his older brother, Dara Shikoh, had on their father. After Dara's defeat, Aurangzeb had him brought back to the city, dirty and in chains, slung over the back of a filthy elephant. If he'd hoped to invite scorn on Dara, it had backfired. People wept in the streets for their lost prince. Furious, Aurangzeb had Dara held down by four men and his head hacked off. It was brought to him on a plate. He had to wash off the filth and blood before he could recognize it.

Age of Literature, Learning, and Death by Elephant

Under the first four "Great Mughals" the arts flourished. Poets, architects, historians, gardeners, and scientists flocked to the courts, and even now many Hindu musicians can trace their roots back to Tansen, a great instrumentalist and singer from the time of Akbar. A famous reworking of one of the world's most ancient (and longest) stories, the *Ramayana*, is still recited in villages by professional storytellers today.

Violence was never far off, however. Criminals were often "sent to the elephant garden", which sounds a lot more peaceful than it was. There, they were executed by elephant – literally trampled to death by nine-ton beasts, trained to either give a quick death or to take their time. Some could even slice a man to death using knives attached to their tusks, but at all times they were under control by their owner, in case the emperor decided to give the victim a last-minute reprieve.

The Last Days of Shah Jahan

The magnificent red sandstone Agra Fort is gigantic, and we don't know exactly how much of it the deposed emperor was allowed to roam. He was allowed servants and his women, but not his freedom.

There were rumours Aurangzeb had his father's food poisoned, a little each day, giving him severe pain and confining him to his bed. The gossip went further, saying he was being massaged with poisoned oils until he wished for death. We have no proof that this actually happened; he does seem to have had severe pains and fever after rubbing his body with *medicated* oil, but by this point the elderly ex-emperor was dying anyway.

Shah Jahan built the Taj Mahal out of love for his wife, Mumtaz Mahal.

Even today, the most haunting parts of the fort are the carefully carved pavilions and windows, through which, it is said, every evening at twilight Shah Jahan would stare wistfully at the dreamlike palace he built for his beautiful Mumtaz.

The End of Religious Tolerance

Aurangzeb's reign saw the end of religious tolerance. He reintroduced the Jazia taxes on non-Muslims, persecuted Muslim sects he didn't agree with, destroyed Hindu temples, and even went as far as torturing and beheading the ninth Sikh Guru. Guru Tegh Bahadar was actually standing up for the rights of *non*-Sikhs, which angered Aurangzeb even more.

This led to serious discontent among people of the many religions of India who had previously coexisted reasonably well. Aurangzeb's extreme orthodoxy led to a much less stable region, and eventually, the weakening of the Mughal Empire. After his reign, things were never the same again. The empire reigned another hundred years, but by the time the British arrived, the once-great Mughals ruled in name only.

JOHN WILKES BOOTH

14 APRIL 1865

Theatregoers, beware of actors bearing grudges — and firearms.

Washington, D.C. was celebrating. **General Robert E. Lee, commander of the Confederate Army of North Virginia, had surrendered four days beforehand; war was almost at an end. President Abraham Lincoln felt he'd earned a trip to the theatre.**

John Wilkes Booth waited until the audience was laughing before pulling the trigger.

What about that comedy everyone was raving about? It was playing at the theatre down the road, and let's face it, they could all do with a laugh. Abe and Mrs. Lincoln invited General Ulysses S. Grant and his wife to join the fun, but when they couldn't come, young Clara Harris and her fiancé, Major Henry Reed Rathbone, stepped in to take the spare tickets.

Halfway through Act III, Scene II, the Lincoln party was chuckling along with the rest of the crowd, unaware that behind them a twenty-six-year-old disenchanted actor, John Wilkes Booth, had a derringer pistol aimed at the president's head. Just when the funniest gag of the show had the audience in stitches, Booth pulled the trigger.

Lincoln collapsed. Booth brandished a knife, stabbed the major, and leaped down onto the stage. The spur of his boot, however, got caught in a flag draped across the box, and he fell, breaking his leg. Booth staggered to his feet, and in the chaos, fled to Mary Surratt's tavern nearby. Dr. Samuel Mudd put his shattered leg into a splint; Booth downed some whisky and disappeared into the night with his friend Davey Herold.

The president was taken to the Petersen boarding house across the street. He died the next day. A manhunt was on.

Twelve days later, Booth and Herold were tracked down to a lonely farm in Virginia. Booth was shot by Sergeant Boston Corbett, aka the Mad Hatter, since he had once cleaned hats for a living. Booth died on the farm porch.

Abraham Lincoln

When Abraham Lincoln was elected sixteenth president of the United States in November 1860, seven slave-owning states (correctly) believed he would end slavery. They broke away from the Union in what's known as "secession" and were later joined by four more.

The northern states believed secession was unconstitutional. The abolition of slavery was also crucial to both the northern states and Lincoln himself. As president, he was honour-bound to maintain the Union and ensure the freedom of all men, by force if necessary.

Confederates attacked the Union's Fort Sumter, and Lincoln knew the moment had come. He called for 75,000 volunteers in what was to become a vicious, complex, and horrifying conflict.

The American Civil War – where the "slave states" in the South, also known as the "Confederacy", fought the loyal states of the North – raged until 1865. Well over a million people died, either as direct casualties or from disease.

When Lincoln was re-elected in 1864, he tried to persuade the Southerners to rejoin the Union, but the wounds were still too fresh. After his assassination, hopes of a swift reconciliation dimmed even further.

Abraham Lincoln

John Wilkes Booth

John Wilkes Booth was born into a famous theatrical family. He too, became an actor, along with his older brothers, Edwin and Junius Brutus Junior.

Edwin especially was a rival in more ways than one. The two brothers vied for attention in the theatre. Edwin is regarded by many as one of America's finest-ever stage actors, but he has forever lived in the shadow of his brother's actions. He was a staunch Unionist as opposed to John Wilkes' Confederate beliefs.

John Wilkes was a handsome man, swooned over by the ladies and popular for his Shakespearean speeches, but he became more and more convinced Abraham Lincoln was responsible for the sufferings of the South. He'd originally intended to just kidnap the president, but he later decided to go the whole way and just murder him instead.

We still have many of Booth's possessions – the boot cut from his broken leg so it could be set, his derringer pistol, knife, map, whistle, compass, keys, and most illuminating of all, his diary. It tells us he was stunned when he heard himself described as a common cutthroat – he truly believed he'd be hailed as a hero. The last entry reads: "I struck for my country and that alone".

Our American Cousin

It was the perfect choice of play for a celebrating president. *Our American Cousin* showed a redneck American "cousin" claiming his inheritance: an English country estate. The laughs were originally written for the actor playing the cousin, but another actor who'd only been given a small role stole the show instead.

E. A. Sothern played a ridiculous English aristocrat called Lord Dundreary, and he shamelessly milked the part. He wore outrageous clothes, a stupid haircut, and very silly sideburns. He put on funny voices and ad-libbed constantly. By the time Lincoln visited, even though Sothern wasn't on, Lord Dundreary had become the character everyone came to see.

As an actor, Booth realized how useful this could be. He knew the play intimately, and best of all, he knew the funniest lines. He chose one the audience was guaranteed to laugh at and shot Lincoln in that split second, hoping the guffawing would cover the blast.

Caesar Complex

It might be completely coincidental that John Wilkes Booth's father, Junius Brutus Booth, was named after one of the world's most notorious assassins (see page 28), but the son certainly lived up to the name.

John Wilkes and his brothers, Junius Brutus Junior and Edwin, appeared on stage together in Shakespeare's play *Julius Caesar* the year before the assassination, and after he shot Lincoln, he allegedly cried, "*Sic semper tyrannis!*" which means "Thus always to tyrants!" The phrase is also rumoured to have been shouted by the ancient Roman, Marcus Junius Brutus, as he stabbed Julius Caesar.

Booth imagined himself as the Roman avenger to the very end. On the run, he wrote in his diary he was being hunted like a dog for doing something Brutus was honoured for.

John Wilkes Booth appeared in Julius Caesar *with his brothers, Junius and Edwin.*

The Bloody Porch

The night tobacco farmer Richard Garrett took in two "wounded soldiers" was also the beginning of his family's downfall. He couldn't refuse help, but he was suspicious the men might be horse thieves. He alerted local Unionists – who set his barn on fire to smoke out the fugitives. It almost instantly lost the poor man's livelihood.

Later, the courts didn't believe the Garretts had never met Booth and refused any compensation. Everyone disliked them – Northerners suspected they'd helped a traitor; Southerners said they'd betrayed a hero.

For years it was said the porch where Booth died showed bloodstains every time it rained. So many souvenir hunters came snooping that the family had to refloor the porch, but the farm – and the family's fortunes – were on the slide.

Ever the showman, Booth was furious at the amount of money being offered for his capture. Only $140,000? It should be at least half a million! He'd be even more offended today to know the place where he met his death is now sandwiched in the middle of a four-lane highway.

World's Worst Bodyguard?

It was well known that John Frederick Parker was an absolute a joke of a policeman. He was often drunk on duty and regularly fell asleep in streetcars when he was supposed to be working.

On the night he was "guarding" the entrance to the president's theatre box, Parker went to the box next door to get a better view. He disappeared altogether during the intermission to a nearby tavern with Lincoln's footman and coach driver.

At his trial for neglect of duty, Parker claimed the president had given him the rest of the night off, and of course no one could prove he hadn't. The incompetent bodyguard was not only let off the hook, but he even kept his job at the White House. He was eventually fired for falling asleep on duty again.

John Wilkes Booth jumped from the Presidential Box at the theatre, breaking his leg

Ford's Theatre

Ford's Theatre started life as a Baptist church, but it was transformed into a swanky palace of entertainment by impresario John T. Ford. Ford was a friend of Booth's, which is how the killer got inside so easily. Lincoln's assassination was also the kiss of death for the theatre. It was immediately closed – banned from ever being used as a place of entertainment again. Ford was paid $88,000 in compensation, but he was furious, especially when it was alleged *he* might have had anything to do with the shooting. He hadn't.

The building languished as a records office and warehouse. People whispered it was cursed, especially when the front collapsed in 1893, killing twenty-two people.

There's a happy ending, though. In 1968, the theatre reopened for all to visit – or even see a show.

Booth's main co-conspiritors were hanged.

Co-Conspirators

Booth's main co-conspirators were quickly rounded up.

Though tavern owner Mary Surratt protested her innocence to the end, she became the first woman ever executed by the federal government.

Davey Herold, a pharmacist's assistant originally recruited to help kidnap the president rather than kill him, gave himself up when the soldiers set the Garretts' barn on fire.

Lewis Powell was a quiet boy nicknamed "Doc" because he looked after sick animals. He'd been tasked by Booth to kill the secretary of state. His gun misfired, so he stabbed William Seward instead, but still failed to kill him.

George Atzerodt was also in on the original kidnapping plan because he knew the local rivers and creeks. He was supposed to kill the vice president, but he had no taste for murder and didn't even try.

All four were hanged at the gallows of the Old Penitentiary at Fort McNair near Washington, D.C., on 7 July 1865. The doctor who had put Booth's leg in a splint escaped execution by one vote.

THE SPANISH INQUISITION

Religious persecution had been rife for millennia, but the Papal Inquisition took it to new heights of horror.

In early medieval times, many Spanish Jews got fed up with being constantly persecuted and reluctantly "converted" to Christianity. The Catholic Church, however, didn't believe them. It was convinced that the *conversos* still practised their religion in secret.

Papal detectives whisper to each other in a Church.

The Inquisition was set up to investigate the crime of heresy, punishing "wicked" people who went against the beliefs of the Church. It wasn't just *conversos* who were targeted. Most of the Inquisition's fury was directed at Jews, but suspected witches, blasphemers (people who insulted God), bigamists (people who married more than once), Muslims, and the very few Protestants who dared live in Spain were all included in the roundup.

By the end of the thirteenth century, the Papal Inquisition had its own prisons, torture chambers, and detectives. *Conversos* tried to escape, but they were caught and sent back to Seville. Soon the dungeons were overflowing. Even a citywide plague couldn't stop the arrests.

The Holy Office couldn't be seen to be making mistakes by arresting innocent people, so they always found *something* people had done wrong, even if it wasn't outright heresy.

Trials were conducted in secret, but the punishments for anyone convicted were anything but hidden.

The lightest penance saw victims forced to bring a rod into church each week, where the priest would whip them in front of the entire congregation. The heaviest involved being burned alive in front of the entire town. Unbelievably, it was called being "relaxed"!

If someone "repented" quickly enough, they could return to daily life, but only after they'd named names of other sinners. Anyone could accuse anyone, completely anonymously. People used the Inquisition to settle old scores, get rid of business rivals, and wreak revenge on neighbours. It bred a culture of fear and intimidation, even among people who felt they had done nothing wrong.

Tomás de Torquemada

The Dominican order of friars preached against heresy and was known as the Hounds of the Lord. Tomás de Torquemada, aka The Black Legend, was the most merciless, fanatical, and sadistic "hound" of all.

Torquemada actually had *converso* relatives; perhaps that made him hate Jews all the more. As the queen's confessor, he'd enjoyed setting up the Inquisition, but on becoming Spain's first Inquisitor General, he set about his work with gusto. He quickly became the most feared man in the land, centralizing the institution and formulating special procedures.

After a while, Torquemada changed from convicting *conversos* to attacking practicing Jews. They were given four months to leave Spain, forced to sell up at derisory sums, but not allowed to take gold or silver out of the country. Despite vows of poverty, Torquemada and the other inquisitors made vast fortunes from fines and confiscated property.

King Ferdinand and Queen Isabella wanted to make Spain as Christian as possible.

King Ferdinand and Queen Isabella

When Ferdinand of Aragon married Isabella of Castile, the two kingdoms were united. They set about making Spain as Christian as possible.

A man in love with a beautiful young *conversa* snuck into her house but discovered, to his shock, the family celebrating a Jewish holiday. The queen was outraged and sent to Rome to get the pope to agree to root out heresy in Castile. The pope agreed, but he was soon horrified at the number of innocent people being condemned without legitimate proof and retracted his permission. The king declared the pope was interfering in Spain's affairs and made him reverse the new decision.

Because they'd recently won an expensive war, the monarchs no longer needed the money they'd been lent by their practicing Jewish subjects, so they could afford to dispense with them. A courtier offered them a lot of cash to be lenient, but Tomás de Torquemada stormed in, pelting the king and queen with thirty pieces of silver and accusing them of betraying Christ.

In 1492, Ferdinand and Isabella waved farewell to one Christopher Columbus as he left for America. In the same year, 200,000 loyal Jews were expelled from Spain.

Trial

The Inquisition court, interrogating the accused.

Conversos languished in prison for weeks, months, sometimes years. Everything was kept secret from them, including their crime!

When they were finally dragged before the inquisitor, they were interrogated about their family and faith and forced to recite the catechism to prove they knew it.

Then came the tricky part.

They had to admit to the judge what they were guilty of. Not knowing wasn't good enough. Sometimes they "admitted" to the wrong thing – something other than heresy. Brilliant – even more to condemn them!

The Inquisition presumed everyone was guilty. It was up to individuals to prove they were innocent. The inquisitor wanted confessions, and no defence, excuses, denials, or explanations would do. Prisoners could reject witnesses, but since they didn't know who their accusers were, they had to give the court a list of people they thought didn't like them.

And worst of all? The victim paid for his own investigation. His property was seized on his arrest.

Torture

Torture was officially the last resort. The masked torturers were forbidden from shedding blood, so they had to be inventive.

Thumbscrews kept the body *sort of* whole. White-hot pincers cauterized the blood as they opened the flesh, so that was all right, too. *Toca* saw water

A Spanish Inquisition torture chamber.

forced into the victim's mouth so they thought they were drowning. No blood. The rack just stretched people 'til their limbs popped, so no blood there, either. In *la garrucha* the victim's hands were tied, and then they were hung by the wrists, with weights on their feet. Every so often they were suddenly dropped, breaking a bone or two. If there was a *little* blood, or they died, it was their own fault for not telling the truth.

Inquisitors knew people would say anything under torture, so victims signed confessions a couple of days later, during a "pause".

Fashion Parade

All victims had to wear a strange, sack-like garment called a *sanbenito*. They came in different styles.

A yellow *sanbenito* with a red cross wasn't too bad. You had to do public penance – extremely painful but not actually fatal. You'd also sport a fetching pointy hat called a *coroza* and a rope around your neck. The number of knots in it represented the number of lashes your body would be receiving later.

The Inquisitor, putting on a full set of chain mail beneath his cassock.

No one wanted a *samara*, painted with devils, demons, and dragons, with you in the middle, surrounded by flames. You were going to hell – via a slow roast at the stake. If you wore a *fuego revolto,* you were lucky. *Its* flames were upside down, meaning you'd be strangled *before* going in the fire.

Auto da Fé

Auto da Fé literally means "trial of faith". Prisoners would be stored up until there was a nice large batch, then paraded before the crowd wearing *sanbenitos*. They were accompanied by effigies and even the coffins of prisoners who'd died waiting for execution. They would then suffer humiliation and public penance, with priests constantly haranguing them to repent.

Autos da Fé got grander and grander, with terraced seating, carpets, and candles for the gentry. A noble might commission an *auto da fé* to celebrate a family member's recovery from illness.

The authorities didn't want a scandal, so the inquisitor's handbook recommended tying the tongues of prisoners who might try to speak.

AMERICAN GANGSTERS

Dangerous job, gangster. If you don't get shot by the feds, chances are you'll be ratted out by your own men.

Legs Diamond, aka Gentleman Jack

Badly nicknamed "Gentleman" Jack, "Legs" Diamond was the gangster that other gangsters didn't trust. He started out as a street thug, graduating to hijacker, bootlegger, kidnapper, torturer, murderer, and double-crosser.

Legs enjoyed the good life, drinking, clubbing, and dancing with showgirls. He was called "Legs" either for his dancing skills or because he was so fast getting away from his enemies. He outlived four assassination attempts – twelve bullets in all – and even managed to stay out of jail after publicly murdering people in his Hotsy Totsy nightclub. He just intimidated all the witnesses so no one would say a word against him.

One night he went out drinking with his girlfriend to celebrate being found "not guilty" yet again. Legs returned home leg-*less,* and the next day he was found shot dead. No one knows who did it, but would-be suspects were told to get in line...

Public Enemy Number One

John Dillinger has a romantic image as a Robin Hood character. He was charming, good-looking, and charismatic – just the sort of outlaw ordinary people who had lost everything in the Great Depression could identify with. He robbed banks. He stole cars. He lived a fast, dangerous life, running around with glamourous girlfriends and tommy guns. He escaped from jail three times, once using a wooden gun blackened with boot polish. His face was all over the papers and the newsreels. That made him almost like a film star, didn't it?

In reality all the bad parts about Dillinger's story were true; all the good parts weren't. He and his gang shot anyone who got in their way but used innocent bystanders as human shields against police bullets. Public Enemy Number One certainly didn't give to the poor any of the money he robbed from the rich.

None of that mattered to his fans. Five thousand people came to stare at John Dillinger's bullet-ridden body after he was finally killed in a showdown with the FBI. His coffin was encased in concrete to deter souvenir hunters, but his headstone had to be replaced several times.

Bugsy Siegel

Called Bugsy because he was "crazy as a bedbug", Benjamin Siegel might have been a handsome, flamboyant crook-about-town who hobnobbed with movie stars and politicians, but he had a very dark side indeed.

Teenage Bugsy started out collecting protection money from market traders. If they asked what they were being protected from, he set fire to their stalls.

Siegel got into bootlegging and soon became the go-to guy for any mobster who wanted someone rubbed out. As part of Murder Incorporated, a murder-to-measure service, he is rumoured to have killed thirty thugs.

Bugsy had a dream, though: Las Vegas. His hotel, the Flamingo, built using mob money, became the blueprint for the entire city.

His problem? He got greedy and started siphoning off wise-guys' cash. He should have known better from his old "protection" days. In 1947, the gangland bosses got together and had their old hit-man hit.

Lucky Luciano

Charles Luciano was great at evading arrest, winning dice games – and surviving assassination attempts. He even lived after a notorious "one-way ride" where he was abducted, beaten up, stabbed with an ice pick, had his throat cut, and was left to die on a deserted beach. No wonder they called him Lucky. Virtually no one who came into contact with him was so fortunate.

It's often said Luciano was the father of organized crime in America, and he started young. By the age of ten, he was already shoplifting, mugging, and extorting cash. He was particularly good at arranging the assassinations of other mobsters. He founded his own crime family, and even after being sent to jail, he continued to rule the underworld.

Amazingly, he died of natural causes!

Bugs Moran

It was no secret that vicious gangster George "Bugs" Moran hated his rival bootlegger, Al Capone, and the feeling was mutual. Both gangs were trying to supply the same speakeasies with their illegal booze. There were scores of casualties on both sides in the deadly turf-war shoot-outs, and innocent bystanders often got hit too.

When his North Side Gang was lured to a warehouse and shot by men wearing police uniforms on 14 February 1929, Bugs was outraged. By the time the real police arrived, six of his men were dead, and another was dying.

Bugs broke the Gangsters' Code. He squealed to the police that Al Capone was responsible for the St. Valentine's Day Massacre.

It did him no good. Capone had the authorities in his pocket, and no one was ever convicted for the murders. Moran never really regained his former power and spent the rest of his life in and out of prison.

Scarface

Possibly the most infamous of all hoodlums, Al Capone was a larger-than-life character who loved good living almost as much as he loved a good fight. Usually he could silence his rivals, enemies – and the law – by bribing them, driving them out of town, or just plain shooting them, but there was one base he hadn't covered. Ultimately, Al Capone was accidentally betrayed by his accountant!

During a routine raid, US Treasury agents discovered Capone's books. They were written in code, but it was so bad that it was easy to figure out what the code meant. Capone had made sure he couldn't be touched on his bootlegging, violence, murder, and corruption, but he hadn't counted on being caught for not paying his taxes...

INDEX

Numbers in bold indicate that an image of the subject will be found on the page.

GLOSSARY

amphitheatre
a semi-circular open-air area used for entertainments and sports in Roman times

Aztecs
warrior tribe of central Mexico

bootlegging
illegal making and selling alcohol, such as in American Prohibition

Buddhists
followers of Buddhism, a religion which features meditation and personal development

canonization
declaration by the Church that a person is a saint and included in the canon (or list) or saints

catechism
in Christian religion this is religious instruction in the form of questions and answers

coffers
a strongbox or chest to hold money or other valuable items

conquistadors
conquerors of new territory, especially 16th-century Spanish and Portuguese soldiers who conquered the New World

court masques
extravagant theatrical entertainment at the Stuart court

derring-do
daring deeds

dictator
a person who rules a country with complete power, and sometimes cruelly

doctored
falsifying the appearance of a document

epitaph
an inscription on a grave in memory of the person who is buried there

FBI (Federal Bureau of Investigation)
US intelligence and security service, concerned with law enforcement at home and abroad

Great Depression (1929-39)
long-lasting economic slump beginning with the Wall Street stock market crash of 1929

heresy
practicing beliefs disagreeing with the established Church

Hindus
people who practise the world religion of Hinduism originating in India

hysteria
a general state of uncontrollable excitement, fear, or panic

Inquisition
courts set up by the Catholic Church to interrogate and punish heresy

Jains
people who practise Jainism, an ancient non-violent Indian religion

Jesuits
members of the Society of Jesus, a Catholic religious order

Jews
people whose traditional faith is the world religion of Judaism. Israel is a Jewish state

litter
human-powered transport such as sedan chairs

Marathas
people from the Indian state of Maharashtra, traditionally landowners and warriors

Mughal Empire
Islamic empire in 16th- and 17th-century India, Pakistan, and Afghanistan

Protestants
followers of a form of Christian faith

Puritans
Protestant Christians who wanted to rid the Church of any Roman Catholic influences

Rajputs
descendants of warrior classes in the Indian subcontinent

regicides
deliberate killers of a monarch

Sikhs
people who practise Sikhism, a world religion founded by Guru Nanak in the Punjab in the 15th century. Their temples are called gurdwaras

soothsayer
someone who claims to predict future events

sorcery
use of magical powers for good or evil

speakeasies
illegal alcohol shops or drinking clubs

toga
a Roman garment, made of wool, which was wrapped around the body over a tunic

vigilantes
people who take the law into their own hands, often with violence

white magic
practitioners who make healing spells for good purposes, whereas in black magic the intentions are evil

ACKNOWLEDGMENTS

Author: Sandra Lawrence

Sandra would like to thank the following
people for their help with this book:

*David Townsend has a rare combination of expertise:
murder, millitary, and maniacs. He was generous with his thoughts
on all three for which I am grateful, in spite of the nightmares.*

*Dr. Dana Huntley's advice on the American chapters was more
valuable than he thinks. I hope he's tickled by the result.*

*My lovely editor Fay Evans kept the faith and always said nice
things about the grimmest stuff. Thank you!*

Illustrator: Bernard Chau

Senior Editor: Fay Evans
Editor: Melissa Brandzel
Designer: Natalie Schmidt
Publisher: Donna Gregory

PICTURE CREDITS: